HOT WORDS
for the
SAT* I

Second Edition

Linda Carnevale, MA
Columbia University, Teachers College

BARRON'S

Dedicated to

my Beloved Sandro
& precious sons Phillip and Andrew
who inspire me daily
~
to my supportive family, friends, colleagues at
Cold Spring Harbor Schools, my wonderful students
~ and ~
to my cherished parents
Anne & Ernest

ACKNOWLEDGMENTS

With love and gratitude to my husband and children, my inspirations. To my husband, who encouraged me every step of the way in this process, through late nights of writing, and who helped me find my way through myriad PC file management debacles.

With love to my parents, Anne and Ernest, who—since I was a pre-schooler—encouraged me to write, and to "dream the impossible dream."

Thanks to my editor, Wendy Sleppin, to Wayne Barr, who first welcomed me to Barron's, and to George Ehrenhaft for his contribution to this book.

All inquiries should be addressed to:
Barron's Educational Series, Inc.
250 Wireless Boulevard
Hauppauge, New York 11788
http://www.barronseduc.com

ISBN-13: 978-0-7641-2314-6
ISBN-10: 0-7641-2314-9

Library of Congress Catalog Card No.: 2003070919

Library of Congress Cataloging-in-Publication Data
Carnevale, Linda.
   Hot words for the SAT I / Linda Carnevale.—2nd ed.
     p.   cm.
   ISBN 0-7641-2314-9
    1. Scholastic Assessment Test—Study guides. 2. English language—Examinations—Study guides. 3. Vocabulary tests—Study guides. I. Title.

   LB2353.57.C357   2004
   378.1′662—dc22   2003070919

Printed in Canada
9 8 7 6 5 4

Contents

Introduction

Are you ready for the HOTTEST of the HOT WORDS?

As a verbal tutor who takes the SAT I several times a year and scores a perfect 800 verbal, I know the words that are most likely to appear. This book is divided into 35 lessons, containing more than 350 SAT I-level words. Additional SAT words are featured in the exercises. For the first time ever, this book contains **Millennium Hot Words**, featuring words that capture some flavor of today's world. These words are likely to appear more and more frequently on the SAT I.

Why is this edition *particularly* HOT?

The innovative format of this edition sets it apart from other vocabulary books. This new format, "**Word Clustering**," is especially effective in learning hundreds of vocabulary words. Unlike dictionary-style, alphabetized lists, Clustering groups Hot Words with similar meanings so that distinctions in usage and connotation can be made more apparent. *Never before presented so comprehensively in an SAT I preparatory book, Clustering boosts vocabulary building exponentially!*

What is expoential vocabulary growth?

Unlike linear growth, which involves a constant addend (+5 in this case)—5-10-15-20-25-30—exponential (or geometric) growth is rapid (×5 in this case)—5-25-125-625-3,125. As you can see, exponential sums far exceed linear sums. Linear vocabulary building involves one isolated, alphabetized word at a time. Exponential vocabulary building involves dynamically associated clusters of words. Consider this visual analogy: Linear vocabulary growth is like a tall stalk of bamboo, adding one foot of bamboo (or one word) at a time. Exponential vocabulary growth is like a massive oak tree, adding whole branches of words at a time.

The majority of lessons in this book are Cluster-formatted so that you can expeditiously learn groups of words at a time. As you work through each Cluster lesson, read the definitions and illustrative sentences carefully. Challenge yourself to learn the nuance or shade of meaning for each individual word in the lesson.

Why cluster vocabulary words?

There are many reasons. Clustering is based on an educational-psychological idea called "apperception." Apperception, according to Merriam-Webster OnLine, is rooted in "the process of understanding something perceived in terms of previous experience." (knowledge) So, for example, if you know that *trite* and *banal* mean "unoriginal," link this "old" knowledge to "new" words like *platitude, hackneyed,* and *cliché.* Moreover, instead of regarding *platitude, hackneyed,* and *cliché* as isolated, unattached elements (as you'd encounter them in an A-B-C order list) think of this trio of words as linked to the same category that already contains *trite* and *banal.* Furthermore, apperception is "perception that reflects upon itself—sometimes intensified or energetic" (Merriam-Webster OnLine). Clustering in this manner keeps you immersed in SAT I–type vocabulary, bringing your vocabulary growth to a new level.

Consider this analogy: Just as teachers of French or Spanish find immersion-style lessons effective, I find SAT I–vocabulary immersion effective for me and for my students. Immerse yourself in SAT I vocabulary. I hope that hearing a particular vocabulary word will bring to mind a bevy—a plethora—of associated words.

In each lesson of *Hot Words,* a connection exists among the words; the words relate to each other in some way. As a verbal tutor, I have seen firsthand how this kind of vocabulary dynamic is highly effective for many of my students. When alphabetized lists are used, confusion and frustration sometimes occur for students because—as you can see— the words may start off in similar ways:

abberation	delectable	rebuff
abridge	delegate	rebuke
abrogate	deleterious	refute
abscond	delineate	rescind
abstain	deluge	revile
abstract	delusion	revoke

These look-alike/sound-alike words tend to get jumbled together, undermining our effort to learn hundreds of SAT I–type words. Alphabetized lists are cumbersome, even trite. Unlike alphabetized lists, *cluster lists* are dynamic. Words that sound and look different can be closely related in meaning. An indispensable benefit of cluster learning is getting a close-up view of the subtleties of difference among the words featured in each lesson. Although challenging, this method is necessary for learning the real sense and usage of words.

Let's talk further about clustering and how this method of learning vocabulary relates to word recall. *Example:* I give you an *alphabetized list* of 25 words to memorize (5 rock bands, 5 sports teams, 5 car brands, 5 fast foods, and 5 colleges). Then I ask you to memorize the list and recite back to me as many terms as you can remember.

Acura	Loyola
BMW	Mets
Cheeseburger	New York University
Columbia University	Nissan
Fried Chicken	NSync
Giants	Pink
Guns n' Roses	Pizza
Harvard University	Rangers
Honda	Soft Pretzel
Hot Dog	Sting
Jaguar	The Cure
Jets	University of Richmond
Knicks	

How would you, personally, recall and recite these 50 terms?

Version A
Alphabetical

Acura	Loyola
BMW	Mets
Cheeseburger	New York University
Columbia University	Nissan
Fried Chicken	NSync
Giants	Pink
Guns n' Roses	Pizza
Harvard University	Rangers
Honda	Soft Pretzel
Hot Dog	Sting
Jaguar	The Cure
Jets	University of Richmond
Knicks	

Version B
Random

Jets	Pink
Soft Pretzel	Hot Dog
Acura	Jaguar
Loyola	Harvard University
Guns n' Roses	Mets
Nissan	Giants
Fried Chicken	NSync
Sting	Cheeseburger
The Cure	New York University
Rangers	Knicks
Honda	University of Richmond
BMW	Columbia University
Pizza	

Version C
Clustered

Jets	Loyola	Jaguar
Knicks	University of Richmond	BMW
Giants	Columbia University	Honda
Mets	New York University	Nissan
Rangers	Harvard University	Acura

Pizza	The Cure
Soft Pretzel	Pink
Hot Dog	Sting
Fried Chicken	Guns n' Roses
Cheeseburger	NSync

For the most part, our brains work and think by associating things that are alike. Clusters and categories are natural to us in terms of how the majority of us learn. Think back to preschool. Did you learn about colors, shapes, and animals simultaneously? Or, did you learn colors, then shapes, then animals, then letters, and so on. Effective learning is not a staccato, haphazard, mumbo-jumbo process that just happens to occur in A-B-C order. Learning is ordered in a way that makes sense.

As you will see as you work through this book, cluster lessons are not made of pure synonyms. Yes, the words relate to a theme or general idea, but the lists compel you to learn the subtle differences in usage and their nuances of meaning. The three illustrative sentences provided with each word, help you to do just this. Based on my students' oral and written testimony to me, week after week, I am convinced that clustering is more effective than basic alphabetized lists.

Clusters are effective. If clustered or theme-based vocabulary is new to you, I suggest you try the bonus section that this revision of *Hot Words* contains: Mini–Vocabulary Clusters (see Appendix A). These bite-size groups of related words will familiarize you with the cluster concept and warm you up for the lessons that contain larger groups of theme-related words.

Memory Tips is a popular and exciting part of *Hot Words*. Toward the end of each lesson, I show you how to capitalize on your memory and how to harness the meanings of a plethora of SAT I words. *Hot Words* shows you practical memory techniques (known as mnemonics) that you can apply to your vocabulary building. Memory Tips show you how resourcefulness and creativity can help you amass a large, upper-level vocabulary.

Research shows that memory works predominantly by linking something new or unknown to some knowledge that you already have. Linking an SAT word (the unknown) to some word you already know is an effective method for the daunting task of learning hundreds of upper–level words. Many Memory Tips work this way—by linking the *new* to the *known*. Other tips, as you'll see, use additional approaches that are just as effective. Some examples are Letter Clusters, Word Roots, Prefixes/Suffixes, Slant Rhymes, Word Pictures, and Chants.

In addition to Millennium Hot Words and Memory Tips, this edition includes **SAT I-Style Analogies** *in every lesson*. Analogies provide excellent vocabulary drills. Furthermore, it makes sense to familiarize yourself with a question format that comprises about a third of the verbal portion of the actual SAT I.

As you work through each lesson, *read aloud* the words, definitions, and sample sentences so that your auditory learning mode is engaged. Be aware of making distinctions in meaning between words that have similar definitions. Try using the words in sentences that you make up on your own.

What role will vocabulary play in the New SAT, scheduled for March 2005?

Vocabulary, in my estimation, will be more important than ever. Because the New SAT will ask students to compose a "writing sample," students' vocabulary skills will matter a great deal. The College Board plans to have students write a persuasive-type essay—and an effective and compelling expository essay requires a strong, rich vocabulary.

A new vocabulary? The College Board plans to feature a fiction excerpt on the New SAT, requiring students to know the vocabulary of literary terms, such as hyperbole, metaphor, simile, and personification.

More critical reading questions will be added to the New SAT, although the size of the additional passages will be shorter. The critical reading passages will still be saturated with upper-level vocabulary, and most questions will still contain high-level vocabulary.

Sentence Completions remain, and the levels 3, 4, and 5 questions have answer choices that brim with upper-level vocabulary. Moreover, most questions feature challenging vocabulary within the sentences themselves. More often than not, these vocabulary words function as context clues for the blanks. Not knowing key words that appear within the sentences can hamper your ability to answer correctly.

Analogies will soon be eliminated; still, a strong and vast vocabulary remains a primary requisite for a competitive verbal score. The Analogy Questions remain in this edition for two reasons. First, students taking the test in fall 2004 and in January 2005 will still have the analogy questions. Second, practice with verbal Analogies is a solid way to build vocabulary. Furthermore, analogies will remain on the PSAT. Remember that in the junior year of high school, the PSAT will remain as the National Merit Scholarship Qualifying Test.

Using a Vocabulary Notebook

I suggest that you buy a marble bound or journal-type notebook that you devote to vocabulary building. Pick a notebook whose cover and size appeal to you. I envision your Vocabulary Notebook as a companion to *Hot Words for the SAT I*. I give you **Memory Tips** in every lesson that use a variety of strategies to help you remember words. I suggest that you write the Memory Tips in your Vocabulary Notebook, underlining or highlighting word roots, prefixes, or letter clusters, as shown in the Memory Tips.

Once you get the hang of using memory clues, I challenge you to come up with memory clues of your own. In order to work efficiently, only invent memory clues for words that challenge you. It would be a waste of time to think up memory clues for words that you already know. As you work through each lesson, add the tips I give to your Notebook, and spend some time inventing your own memory devices. After all, you have special knowledge that's unique to you: travel, a foreign language, a hobby, an instrument, and so on. Your "special knowledge" can help you come up with memory tips that no one else can.

Let your Vocabulary Notebook be colorful and lively! Underline or highlight parts of the words in color! Clip vocabulary words that you spot in newspapers and magazines, and paste them into your Notebook. I recommend that you clip and paste the entire phrase or headline, for example, so that the word has a context. Read through the words and tips in your Vocabulary Notebook each day. This ritual will solidify the meanings of new words for you. May you build a strong and vital vocabulary.

Linda Carnevale

<table>
<tr><td>

Lesson 1

</td><td>

CAT GOT YOUR TONGUE?

Words Relating to Using Few Words or Being Quiet

</td></tr>
</table>

---

brevity concise laconic pithy quiescent reticent succinct taciturn terse

---

brevity *n.* briefness or conciseness in speech or writing

For the sake of **brevity**, choose your words with care.

Limited space in the newsletter makes **brevity** essential.

When time is short, **brevity** is a virtue.

concise *adj.* using few words in speaking and writing

A **concise** explanation is preferable to a long-winded one.

Leslie's essay is pretty wordy; she should try to be more **concise**.

For a **concise** summary of the book, read the book jacket.

laconic *adj.* using few words in speech

Because Bush's **laconic** reply lacked specificity, it raised more questions than it answered.

It was just too hot to give more than a **laconic** response to the question.

Ms. Allen's **laconic** explanation consisted of a single word: pepperoni.

pithy *adj.* brief and full of meaning and substance; concise

For the yearbook, Jenny searched through *Bartlett's* for a **pithy** quotation about courage.

Jonathan's sonnet ended with a **pithy** rhyming couplet.

What expresses affection more **pithily** than the three words, *I love you*?

quiescent *adj.* quiet; still; inactive

Mount St. Helens has been **quiescent** since its last eruption in 1986.

On long summer weekends, the city loses its bustle and is strangely **quiescent**.

Never one to make waves, Leo **quiescently** followed the coach's orders.

reticent *adj.* not talking much; reserved

Usually **reticent**, Ms. Worthy surprised us all with a long story at lunch.

Tom and Molly are a mismatched pair; he's shy and **reticent**, while she never stops talking.

I thought the old man was **reticent**, but he wouldn't talk because he had no teeth.

succinct *adj.* clearly and briefly stated; concise

Mr. Phillips asked us to write a **succinct** summary of our term papers.

The title **succinctly** conveys the point of my paper.

Let me state this as **succinctly** as I can: "No late papers."

taciturn *adj.* silent; sparing of words; close-mouthed

Next to me on the bus sat a **taciturn** girl who said nothing during the four-hour ride.

Throughout the party, Larry was moody and **taciturn**. No one heard a peep from him.

Mom kept quiet, not because she's **taciturn**, but because she refused to make the decision for me.

terse *adj.* using only the words that are needed to make the point; very concise, sometimes to the point of rudeness

Mia wanted details about Joyce's new boyfriend, but got only a **terse** description.

Terse speakers make dull lecturers.

The principal's **terse** reply was clear: "No dogs at school."

MEMORY TIPS

Use these mnemonics (memory devices) to boost your vocabulary. Make up your own memory clues for words in this lesson that are challenging for you. Add these two tips—and your own—to your Vocabulary Notebook.

brevity Connect this word to a related word that you most likely already know: **abbreviate**. Notice how both words share the letter cluster *brev*!

pithy Think of just the *pit* (central part) of the topic and nothing more. Remember that **pithy** expressions are substantial and to the point.

quiescent Did you notice that the word *quiet* is within **quiescent**? Use this to *see* the definition within the word: still; inactive; quiet. In your Vocabulary Notebook, underline or highlight q-u-i-e-t in **quiescent**. Another SAT I-level word, ac**quiesce**, is related to **quiescent**. Acquiesce means "to peaceably agree or quietly give in to."

MATCHING

Match the vocabulary words in Column A with *one or more* of their defining characteristics appearing in Column B.

Column A	Column B
1. quiescent	a. inactive or still
2. pithy	b. to the point
3. concise	c. using few words to express oneself
4. terse	d. quiet and reserved
5. taciturn	e. brief, almost to the point of rudeness

SAT I-STYLE ANALOGIES

First, express a clear and concise relationship between the two given terms. Next, select the pair in the answer choices that *most closely* shares a similar relationship.

1. QUIESCENT : LOUD

    a. bold : timid
    b. rude : laconic
    c. grim : serious
    d. elusive : stoic
    e. dogged : fetid

2. GABBY : TACITURN

    a. slim : starving
    b. rigid : pliable
    c. pious : frenetic
    d. subservient : servile
    e. victorious : temperate

3. SUCCINCT : LONG-WINDED

    a. bifold : secondary
    b. repetitive : ironic
    c. weary : novel
    d. onerous : contrite
    e. trite : original

4. CHATTERBOX : RETICENT

    a. imp : pesty
    b. veteran : jaunty
    c. disputant : jumpy
    d. martinet : lax
    e. yoeman : zesty

5. PITHY : HEADLINE

    a. flabby : waistline
    b. crunchy : peanut brittle
    c. lanky : forest
    d. comfy : stool
    e. sprightly : evergreen

WORDS IN CONTEXT

Based on the context in which each **bold** word is used, identify the word usage of each sentence as either C (Correct) or I (Incorrect).

1. The mayor was commended for his **pithy** speech. He made meaningful points during a mere half-hour delivery.

2. The gabby shop owner welcomed **laconic** exchanges with customers.

3. Since space is limited, the advertising executive instructed copywriters to write **concise** photo captions.

4. Unlike their customary drawn-out explanations, the Grants related the story of the burglary **tersely**.

5. **Succinct** gossip is most painful; it hurts its subjects more than any other type of rumor.

Lesson 2

THE RUNAWAY MOUTH
Words Relating to Speaking

bombastic circumlocution colloquial diffuse digress eloquence garrulous grandiloquent loquacious prattle ramble rant rhetorical verbose voluble

bombastic *adj.* using language in a pompous, showy way; speaking to impress others

Luke's speech was so **bombastic**; was he speaking to communicate or simply to show off?

Putting on airs, the **bombastic** orator used a bunch of big words that basically said nothing at all.

"Keep your language simple and honest," urged the English teacher. "**Bombast** in writing or speaking is ostentatious. In other words, high-flown language is unacceptable."

circumlocution *n.* speaking in circles; roundabout speech

To avoid hurting anyone's feelings, Hank resorted to **circumlocution**.

Circumlocution is commonly called *beating around the bush.*

The principal said, "Your **circumlocution** is wasting time. Just tell me exactly what you saw out in the parking lot."

colloquial *adj.* pertaining to common everyday speech; conversational

The book is filled with **colloquial** expressions that reflect the speech of people in the deep South.

Two examples of **colloquial** greetings are "Hey, dude, how's it goin'?" and "What's up, man?"

Sometimes a **colloquial** word becomes standard in English usage.

diffuse *adj.* spread out, not concise; wordy

The class discussion was so **diffuse** that few solid points were made.

"This essay lacks focus," said the teacher. "It's too **diffuse**."

A **diffuse** argument won't convince the class to vote for me.

digress *vb.* to wander off from the subject or topic spoken about

We don't have time to **digress** from the main issue right now.

The **digressions** in Carl's speech interested me more than the main topic.

Mr. Helms habitually **digresses** from the point of the lesson.

eloquence *n.* artful ease with speaking; speech that can impact people's feelings

Even the most **eloquent** graduation speeches are quickly forgotten.

Although he sounds **eloquent**, he still is full of hot air.

Among American presidents, Lincoln wins the prize for **eloquence**.

garrulous *adj.* talkative; loquacious

Garrulous gatherings of students are unwelcome in a library that values silence.

Garrulous merrymakers gather in Times Square on New Year's Eve.

Our sightseeing guide was so **garrulous** that we never got to enjoy the serenity of the mountain lake.

grandiloquent *adj.* using big and fancy words when speaking for the purpose of impressing others

"Instead of **grandiloquence**," cautioned the teacher, "use plain language."

Mr. Green tries to impress students with his **grandiloquence** instead of telling them what they need to know.

Mickey used **grandiloquent** language to conceal his ignorance of the subject.

loquacious *adj.* very talkative; liking to talk; garrulous

The **loquacious** audience grew quiet when the movie started.

Have you ever met a lawyer who wasn't **loquacious**?

Loquacity was not Steve's strength; he was quiet and subdued.

prattle *vb.* to speak on and on in a senseless and silly manner; to talk foolishly

The **prattle** of freshmen resounded through the cafeteria.

"Stop **prattling**," urged Ms. Ham. "I can't understand a word you're saying."

After twenty straight hours in the car, their intelligent conversation turned into **prattle**.

ramble *vb.* to talk on and on pointlessly, without clear direction

Rambling on and on, Harold lost his audience's attention; his listeners had no idea what he was talking about.

The teacher **rambled** endlessly about various unrelated topics.

A wandering, unfocused mind is one trait of a **rambler**.

rant *vb.* to talk very loudly, even wildly

Because the speaker **ranted** on and on, the audience stopped listening after a while.

Upset by plummeting sales, the boss stormed into the office and **ranted** at her sales staff, "We're on the verge of bankruptcy!"

Ranting is far from a polite way to get your point across.

rhetorical *adj.* relating to speech that is used to persuade or have some effect; insincere in expression

The speech of politicians is often thick with **rhetoric**.

The attorney's forceful **rhetoric** convinced the jury to acquit the defendant.

Metaphors, allusions, and pithy quotations are examples of **rhetorical** devices.

verbose *adj.* using too many words; wordy; long-winded

> The teacher asked Brenda to cut her **verbose** speech from forty to fifteen minutes.

> When time is short, **verbose** explanations are inappropriate.

> Some English teachers call **verbose** writing "flabby."

voluble *adj.* talking a great deal with ease; glib

> Victor is such a **voluble** speaker that it takes him a half hour to answer a simple question.

> Sean always has been shy around girls, but he's trying to be more **voluble**.

> Unlike her more **voluble** opponent, Ollie gave short and well-focused speeches during the election campaign.

MEMORY TIPS

Use these mnemonics (memory devices) to boost your vocabulary. Make up your own memory clues for words in this lesson that are personally challenging. Add these two tips—and your own—to your Vocabulary Notebook.

loc-, loq- These word roots relate to speaking. Notice how they appear in five words in this lesson: **circum<u>loc</u>ution, col<u>loq</u>ial, e<u>loq</u>uence, grandi<u>loq</u>uent,** and **<u>loq</u>uacious.**

garrulous Think of "**garrulous** gorillas" in the jungle and how noisy and *talkative* they are! Use "**Garrulous** gorillas! **Garrulous** gorillas! **Garrulous** gorillas!" as an alliterative chant; say it aloud three times in a row! Write this chant three times in your Vocabulary Notebook.

<u>prattle</u> In your mind's eye, picture a baby playing with *rattles* while she **<u>prattles</u>.** Once again, take advantage of the letter clusters (and sometimes words) that naturally occur within the vocabulary words. This visual mnemonic is highly memorable since it creates a fun-loving, even silly, picture in your mind's eye.

voluble Be careful with this word. Do *not* think about volume in terms of loudness of speech; instead, think about volume in terms of *quantity* or *amount* of speech. In other words, Victor can be speaking **volubly** while he is whispering. **Voluble** means glib—not loud. Get it?

MATCHING

Match the vocabulary words in Column A with *one or more* of their defining characteristics appearing in Column B.

Column A	Column B
1. garrulous	a. to speak loudly, almost yelling
2. prattle	b. using many words
3. eloquence	c. emotionally stirring speech
4. rant	d. silly talk
5. voluble	e. very talkative

SAT I-STYLE ANALOGIES

First, express a clear and concise relationship between the two given terms. Next, select the pair in the answer choices that *most closely* shares a similar relationship.

1. PRATTLE : CHILDISH
   a. drivel : suave
   b. chatter : complex
   c. grandiloquence : pompous
   d. joking : limp
   e. song : mirthful

2. RAVE : RANT
   a. clap : drop
   b. swerve : veer
   c. repeat : repel
   d. redirect : return
   e. tune : prune

3. BLABBERMOUTH : VOLUBLE
   a. imp : irritating
   b. visionary : jaunty
   c. disputant : jovial
   d. martinet : uncanny
   e. farmer : inane

4. RESERVED : LOQUACIOUS
   a. kinesthetic : subservient
   b. audacious : enumerated
   c. entitled : directed
   d. delineated : described
   e. civil : impolite

5. ELOQUENCE : ORATOR
   a. stamina : artist
   b. ego : narcissist
   c. humiliation : elder
   d. trepidation : leper
   e. frigidness : jingoist

WORDS IN CONTEXT

Based on the context in which each **bold** word is used, identify the word usage of each sentence as either C (Correct) or I (Incorrect).

1. Deep thought is behind prattling.

2. Contrary to popular belief, ranting is very peaceful.

3. "Verbose speech will be penalized for its long and drawn out character," said the debate coach.

4. Political candidates can benefit from an eloquent manner of speaking.

5. Garrulous partygoers huddled in the den corner, observing the crowd quietly.

Lesson 3

THE HIGH AND MIGHTY
Words Relating to Feeling Superior

arrogant braggart complacent contemptuous disdainful egotistical haughty insolent narcissistic ostentatious presumptuous pretentious supercilious swagger

arrogant *adj.* overbearing; proud; haughty

Peter's **arrogance** annoyed his classmates, who thought him to be vain and conceited.

His **arrogant** attitude made it hard for others to warm up to him.

The dog looked like its master, **arrogant** and proud, not the sort of pet to cuddle with.

braggart *n.* one who boasts a great deal

Leo cannot help being a **braggart**. He boasts all day about his exploits on the basketball court.

Even if you are a champion swimmer, avoid sounding like a **braggart** on your college application essay.

Although Tanya is very proud of her talents, she isn't a **braggart**.

complacent *adj.* self-satisfied; smug

Complacent in his role as an assistant dean, Mr. Rogers did not aspire to become a principal.

Carole could get an A in math, but she's too **complacent** to work for it.

Complacence destroys ambition.

contemptuous *adj.* lacking respect; scornful

Accustomed to filet mignon, Fido glared **contemptuously** at the bowl of dog chow in front of him.

When rival cliques are **contemptuous** of each other, there's going to be trouble.

Parents should teach tolerance, not breed **contempt** for people's differences.

disdainful *adj.* full of bitter scorn and pride; aloof

The audience showed its **disdain** by heckling the singer who couldn't carry a tune.

When asked for a dollar for a cup of coffee, Mrs. Snodbrow eyed the panhandler **disdainfully**.

I can't keep my **disdainful** comments to myself when Emily deliberately acts foolishly to get attention.

egotistical *adj.* excessively self-absorbed; very conceited

Egotistical individuals cannot get enough of their own reflections in the mirror.

Nathan is so **egotistical**; he thinks every girl on campus wants to meet him.

The **egotistical** student could not understand why he was not voted most popular by the senior class.

haughty *adj.* having great pride in oneself and dislike for others

Ralph struts around like a proud rooster. His **haughtiness** keeps him from making friends.

Haughty Hannah has no use for others; she's too busy thinking and talking about herself.

The folks next door are too **haughty** for a Ford; they drive only Mercedes and BMWs.

insolent *adj.* boldly disrespectful in speech or behavior; rude

When Ernie told the principal to "bug off," his **insolence** earned him a suspension from school.

"No **insolent** remarks on the ball field," warned the coach. "Teammates must respect each other, even when they strike out."

Before she met that wild crowd, Megan was quiet and demure. Now she's an **insolent**, foul-mouthed roughneck.

narcissistic *adj.* having to do with extreme self-adoration and a feeling of superiority to everyone

> Becky is so **narcissistic**, she even chooses her friends based on how their looks complement hers.

> Quentin is a full-fledged **narcissist**; he spends half the day in front of a mirror adoring himself.

> Feeling good about yourself is healthy, but when self-esteem turns to **narcissism**, you've got a problem.

ostentatious *adj.* having to do with showing off; pretentious

> Don't you agree that wearing a pearl bracelet, two ruby rings, and diamond-studded earrings is a bit **ostentatious**?

> Meredith talks about nothing but her father's yacht, ski trips to Aspen, Club Med vacations, and other **ostentatious** displays of wealth.

> My parents prefer staying at a quiet inn by the sea to a glitzy, **ostentatious** Miami Beach hotel.

presumptuous *adj.* too forward or bold; overstepping proper bounds

> Isn't it **presumptuous** of Julie to expect all her friends to do only what *she* wants to do on Friday nights?

> **Presumptuous** people would be better off with a bit of self-control and tact.

> On his first day of work, Harris **presumptuously** asked his boss, "When do I get a raise?"

pretentious *adj.* claiming or pretending increased importance; ostentatious; affectedly grand

> My neighbors thrive on **pretension**. They plaster their windshields with the decals of posh prep schools, beach clubs, and Ivy League colleges.

> **Pretentious** Patrick never goes anywhere without a copy of *Ulysses* under his arm, even though he's never read a word of it.

> Isn't **pretension** often a mask for self-doubt?

supercilious *adj.* looking down on others; proud and scornful

> While strutting to class with her nose in the air, **supercilious** Sue notices no one.

> If we held a contest for **superciliousness**, haughty Hannah would win hands down.

> "Success depends on everyone working together as equals," explained Esther. "No one with a **supercilious** attitude is welcome."

swagger *vb.* to walk around in a proud, showy manner; to boast in a loud manner

> Butch's **swagger** reveals an ego as big as a house.

> Walking around the school with his customary **swagger**, Pat conveys the impression that he owns the place.

> Mike and Gloria acted like guests of honor at the party, **swaggering** from room to room.

MEMORY TIPS

Use these mnemonics (memory devices) to boost your vocabulary. Make up your own memory clues for words in this unit that are personally challenging. Add these two tips—and your own—to your Vocabulary Notebook. Remember, vocabulary building is key to increasing your score on the verbal SAT I.

haughty This chant is catchy and helpful: "It's naughty to be **haughty**! It's naughty to be **haughty**! It's naughty to be **haughty**!" Repeated three times in succession, the chant emphasizes the negative connotation of this word. Haughtiness is an undesirable character trait.

narcissistic Have you heard about the good-looking Greek guy named Narcissus? Narcissus falls in love with his own reflection! He stays lakeside forever, gazing adoringly, until he withers and dies. If that isn't self-loving and self-adoring, what is?

pretentious Let the first six letters of this word lead you to its meaning. Think of it this way: **Pretentious** is about pretending to be more than you are. See, it's as if the meaning is built into the vocabulary word!

MATCHING

Match the vocabulary words in Column A with *one or more* of their defining characteristics in Column B. Remember, some words may have more than one correct answer.

Column A	Column B
1. disdainful	a. overly proud; disliking others
2. complacent	b. smug
3. haughty	c. a boastful individual
4. pretentious	d. disrespectful
5. braggart	e. pretending to be more important than you are

SAT I-STYLE ANALOGIES

First, express a clear and concise relationship between the two given terms. Next, select the pair in the answer choices that *most closely* shares a similar relationship.

1. SMUG : COMPLACENT
   a. grand : meek
   b. guileless : timid
   c. honest : forthright
   d. candid : dainty
   e. reclusive : servile

2. PRESUMPTUOUS : UNASSUMING
   a. rotund : listless
   b. merry : unpleasant
   c. amenable : craven
   d. simple : obtuse
   e. audacious : bold

3. ARROGANCE : BRAGGART
   a. serenity : zealot
   b. insincerity : fraud
   c. remoteness : friend
   d. pride : lioness
   e. intelligence : elder

4. PROUD : INSOLENT
   a. firm : dogmatic
   b. maimed : weak
   c. resilient : stubborn
   d. strict : austere
   e. slim : fine

5. BELITTLING : DISDAINFUL
   a. obliging : discordant
   b. robust : glad
   c. edifying : demystifying
   d. shrewd : perspicacious
   e. melancholy : vague

WORDS IN CONTEXT

Based on the context in which each **bold** word is used, identify the word usage of each sentence as either C (Correct) or I (Incorrect).

1. Above all, Mia's supercilious attitude shows her generosity of spirit.

2. Arrogance results from an individual's selflessness.

3. Rudeness is one component of insolence.

4. For the braggart, showiness and pretension go hand in hand.

5. A complacent youth has a great desire to learn from the experience of others.

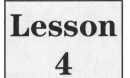

Lesson 4

THAT'S ALL BEEN SAID BEFORE!

Words Relating to Unoriginal, Dull, Played Out

**banal cliché derivative hackneyed insipid lackluster
mundane platitude prosaic trite vapid**

---

banal *adj.* dull or stale because of overuse; trite; hackneyed

To wake up and realize your adventure was all a dream is a **banal** ending for a short story.

Have you heard the **banal** joke about the moron who threw the clock out the window in order to see time fly?

Banality is boring because it's so predictable.

cliché *n.* an idea or expression that has become stale due to overuse

"I'm so hungry I could eat a *rhinoceros*," gives an original twist to an old **cliché**.

Good writers avoid **clichés** like the plague.

Lazy writers rely on **clichés** because it's hard work to express ideas with fresh, new phrases.

derivative *adj.* unoriginal; taken from something already existing

"Write an original sci-fi story," instructed Mr. Schirmer, "not **derivative** fiction drawn from *2001: A Space Odyssey* or *The Time Machine*."

Instead of presenting her unique artistic vision, Julie's **derivative** work resembled the paintings of the old masters.

English is a **derivative** language. It is made up of words from many other languages.

hackneyed *adj.* made commonplace by overuse; trite

> Miss Cole, our poetry teacher, said, "Because poets aim to create new insights, they shun **hackneyed** language."

> Then she added, "If you think imaginatively, you'll avoid **hackneyed** phrases such as *ruby lips* and *rosy-fingered dawn.*"

> Only hack writers rely on **hackneyed** expressions. That's what makes them hacks.

insipid *adj.* lacking flavor or taste; unexciting

> The conversation at dinner was so **insipid** that Monica fell asleep at the table.

> What kept the Hagans from going to church on Sunday morning was the minister, whose **insipid** sermons made them want to go back to bed.

> What I thought would be a scary movie turned out to be an **insipid** story of a harmless ghost.

lackluster *adj.* lacking vitality, energy, or brightness; boring

> Laura's **lackluster** grades may prevent her from going to a top college.

> **Lackluster** teachers, who can't engage their students' interest, give this school a bad name.

> Even a superior actor can't enliven a **lackluster** script.

mundane *adj.* commonplace; ordinary

> In contrast to the new and unusual, the **mundane** happenings of everyday existence are pretty dull.

> Woolf is an author who can find something magical even in such a **mundane** activity as brushing one's teeth.

> The movies offer an escape from the **mundane** character of daily life.

platitude *n.* quality of being dull; an obvious remark uttered as if it were original

> How Rick's poem won an award for originality boggles my mind, for it consists of nothing but **platitudes**.

A **platitude** is as enriching intellectually as last month's bread is satisfying nutritionally.

A recipe to induce sleep is a monotonous voice and a plethora of **platitudes**.

prosaic *adj.* dull; commonplace

The novel *Mr. and Mrs. Bridge* is an indictment of an ordinary American couple who lead the dullest, most **prosaic** life imaginable.

A **prosaic** Sunday morning means sleeping late and lingering over a big pancake breakfast while browsing the Sunday newspaper.

What is more **prosaic** than a movie and pizza on a Friday night?

trite *adj.* unoriginal and stale due to overuse

Because my essay was filled with clichés, Mr. Gill red-penciled "**trite**" all over it.

When Bob asked what I thought of getting up at 4 A.M., only the **tritest** response came to me: "Well, they say the early bird catches the worm."

Mr. Gill claims that **triteness** is a sign of an air-filled brain.

vapid *adj.* lacking freshness and zest; flat; stale

Behind every uninspiring, **vapid** TV sit-com you'll find an empty-headed producer, director, and screenwriter.

Tired of **vapid** advertising gimmicks, the company resorted to sky-writing to promote its newest line of swimwear.

The speaker's **vapid** delivery emptied the conference hall within 10 minutes.

MEMORY TIPS

Use these mnemonics (memory devices) to boost your vocabulary. Make up your own memory clues for words in this lesson that are personally challenging. Add these two tips—and your own—to your

Vocabulary Notebook. Remember, vocabulary building is key to increasing your score on the verbal SAT I.

banal You can spell *bla* from **banal**, right? Now, let *bla* be the connection to boring; *boring* is one solid definition for **banal**.

lackluster The two components of this compound word—*lack* and *luster*—literally convey this word's sense: without shine or brilliance. Now recall **lackluster's** extended meanings, including uncreative, unoriginal, and so on.

MATCHING

Match the vocabulary words in Column A with *one or more* of their defining characteristics appearing in Column B.

Column A

1. lackluster
2. prosaic
3. cliché
4. vapid
5. banal
6. platitude

Column B

a. a trite saying; banality
b. without zest or flavor
c. without brilliance or originality
d. unoriginal
e. overused expression
f. very boring, drawn out

SAT I-STYLE ANALOGIES

First, express a clear and concise relationship between the two given terms. Next, select the pair in the answer choices that most closely shares a similar relationship.

1. HACKNEYED : NOVELTY

   a. rigid : durability
   b. curtailed : need
   c. glib : succinctness
   d. recalcitrant : warmth
   e. noble : newness

2. SAYING : PLATITUDE

   a. expression : banality
   b. ego : humility
   c. talent : sterility
   d. flavor : civility
   e. event : reality

3. COPYCAT : CLICHÉS

   a. dilettante : nuances
   b. heretic : prayers
   c. autocrat : admonitions
   d. insurgent : redundancies
   e. tyro : whispers

4. INGENUITY : TRITENESS

   a. enmity : affection
   b. resilience : humor
   c. egoism : aversion
   d. substance : jargon
   e. whimsy : goodness

5. INSIPID : INVENTIVE

   a. benign : fervid
   b. obtuse : keen
   c. colloquial : crass
   d. vivid : inane
   e. dire : repetitive

WORDS IN CONTEXT

Based on the context in which each **bold** word is used, identify the word usage of each sentence as either C (Correct) or I (Incorrect).

1. A **vapid** story is something new under the sun.

2. "As white as snow" is not an example of a **banality**.

3. **Cliché** phrasing substantially bolsters the emotional impact of poetry.

4. An expression that "rings a bell" is likely to be considered **hackneyed**.

5. **Trite** essay titles are likely to grab a reader's attention.

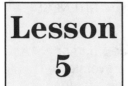

Lesson 5

MAKING THINGS BETTER BUNCH

Words Relating to Lessening Pain, Tension, and/or Conflict

---

allay alleviate ameliorate appease assuage conciliate
mediate mitigate mollify pacify placate quell

---

allay *vb.* to lessen fear; to calm; to relieve pain

An SAT prep course can **allay** the anxiety of some students, but can heighten tension for others.

The recorded sound of waterfalls and breaking waves is said to **allay** stress.

In order to **allay** Allen's worries about his grade in chemistry, Ms. Petrie told him to expect at least an A-minus.

alleviate *vb.* to lessen pain or tension

Grandma takes pills to **alleviate** her arthritic pain.

To **alleviate** overcrowding, the school administration proposes running two class schedules, one early and one late.

A long soak in a hot tub can **alleviate** the tensions of the day.

ameliorate *vb.* to make better; to lessen pain, difficulty, or tension

Marv takes time every day to **ameliorate** the stress of school and work; he takes walks, jogs, gets a massage, or listens to the Grateful Dead.

The doctor prescribed a new ointment to **ameliorate** the rash on my legs.

Side air bags **ameliorate** some of my anxiety about driving a small car.

appease *vb.* to make tranquil or quiet, especially by giving into demands; to pacify

Albert comes to French class late most days. Yesterday he tried to **appease** his teacher by bringing her a burrito and a soda.

Madame Goldbrick was amused but not **appeased**, so Albert's grade suffered.

What did Albert do to **appease** his parents? He offered to cook them a gourmet dinner.

assuage *vb.* to alleviate; to lessen pain or conflict; pacify

If you bake yourself in the sun, try aloe vera gel to **assuage** the pain of sunburn.

Listening to my tale of woe may help to **assuage** your own troubles.

To help Hildy **assuage** her anger, Tom sat her down and let her vent for a while.

conciliate *vb.* to win a person over through special considerations or persuasive methods

Hoping to end the argument, Judd offered a **conciliatory** handshake to his adversary.

To ease the tensions between the two countries, the prime minister made a **conciliatory** speech on TV.

He toned down the harsh language with some **conciliatory** words such as "sorry" and "please."

mediate *vb.* to act as a go-between in settling conflicts or disputes between people or opposing sides

Hal is impartial. That is why he's a good man to **mediate** between the two gangs.

Unless we get a **mediator** who can bring the sides together, the strike won't end until next Christmas.

To be an effective **mediator**, it helps to have experience in resolving conflicts.

mitigate *vb.* to make or become less severe; to lessen pain or damage

A sudden shift in the wind **mitigated** the intensity of the storm.

To **mitigate** the pain in her sore throat, Ellie drank a cup of mint tea with honey.

Ms. Walsh **mitigated** her students' worries about the SAT I by holding a review class after school.

mollify *vb.* to pacify, soothe, or appease; to make less severe or violent

Jay **mollified** his mother by bringing home all A's on his report card.

I tried to comfort her with hugs, but she wouldn't be **mollified** so easily.

Not even the offer of a free ticket could **mollify** Greg's anger after the airline lost his suitcase.

pacify *vb.* to calm; to make peaceful; to restore to a tranquil state

After wrecking the family car, Maura tried to **pacify** her parents with a bouquet of daisies.

Mother **pacified** her crying baby by rubbing his tummy.

The unruly crowd refused to be **pacified** by speeches promising better days in the future.

placate *vb.* to make calm; to soothe

What can be done to **placate** impatient drivers caught in a traffic jam?

Don't try to **placate** me by telling me you'll change in the future. Change now!

The restaurant tried to **placate** us with free appetizers after a one-hour wait for a table.

quell *vb.* to pacify; to subdue; to quiet down

Having been tipped off, the police managed to **quell** the disturbance.

Shouting "Quiet!" failed to **quell** the noise in the auditorium.

A night-light helped to **quell** the baby's fear of the dark.

MEMORY TIPS

Use these mnemonics (memory devices) to boost your vocabulary. Make up your own memory clues for words in this lesson that are personally challenging. Add these two tips—and your own—to your Vocabulary Notebook. Remember, vocabulary building is key to increasing your score on the verbal SAT I.

Notice that both mnemonics below use a technique called "Letter Clusters." As the following examples illustrate, Letter Clusters are naturally-occurring groups of letters within the vocabulary word that offer hints to the word's meaning.

alleviate Let the first five letters, *allev*, rhyme with *relieve*, which is a condensed definition of **alleviate**.

appease Let the last five letters, *pease*, remind you of *peace*. Link that to the overall meaning of this word, to make peaceful.

assuage Have you ever heard of a slant rhyme? Slant rhymes are imperfect rhymes, whereby the words sound similar—but not exactly the same. One of my favorite memory tips is using a slant rhyme between **assuage** and **massage**. As you know, massage is often used to alleviate tension. Can you see how the meaning of massage relates to your vocabulary word **assuage**?

MATCHING

Match the vocabulary words in Column A with *one or more* of their defining characteristics appearing in Column B.

Column A

1. conciliate
2. mitigate
3. pacify
4. quell
5. alleviate

Column B

a. to make calm

b. to lessen fear and anxiety

c. to soothe

d. to make quiet; to settle down

e. to win someone over

SAT I-STYLE ANALOGIES

First, express a clear and concise relationship between the two given terms. Next, select the pair in the answer choices that *most closely* shares a similar relationship.

1. RELIEVE : ALLEVIATE

    a. invent : devise
    b. handle : exhibit
    c. tell : rescind
    d. narrate : bridle
    e. design : gerrymander

2. QUELL : AMPLIFY

    a. undo : lessen
    b. yodel : linger
    c. abridge : extend
    d. quiet : impede
    e. joust : rival

3. MEDIATOR : MITIGATE

    a. neonate : idealize
    b. sonneteer : forecast
    c. imp : hike
    d. soprano : compose
    e. runner : sprint

4. AGGRAVATE : ALLEVIATE

    a. lampoon : deride
    b. indulge : divulge
    c. usurp : implore
    d. beseech : heed
    e. aggrandize : lessen

5. MOLLIFY : CALM

    a. ascend : detract
    b. contract : distend
    c. invert : transfer
    d. twist : tear
    e. narrate : tell

WORDS IN CONTEXT

Based on the context in which each **bold** word is used, identify the word usage of each sentence as either C (Correct) or I (Incorrect).

1. To quell a tumultuous situation, one must first question those involved.

2. For some, listening to the rhythms of waterfalls can help to assuage strain and anxiety.

3. Once several burdens were lessened, Jessica's anxiety was alleviated.

4. The agitators tried to mollify the stressed-out shoppers.

5. How can adults be expected to remember how our testing anxieties were best pacified by our parents and teachers?

Review Exercises / Lessons 1–5

NAME THAT CLUSTER

To the left of the groups of words, put the Roman numeral that corresponds with these theme (or cluster) titles:

Words Relating to . . .

I. Feeling Superior
II. Dull, Unoriginal, Played Out
III. Lessening Pain, Tension, and/or Conflict
IV. Using Few Words or Being Quiet
V. Speaking

Cluster Title _____ 1. loquacious, garrulous, rant, prattle, voluble
Cluster Title _____ 2. assuage, ameliorate, quell, placate, alleviate
Cluster Title _____ 3. hackneyed, trite, mundane, derivative, banal
Cluster Title _____ 4. haughty, braggart, swagger, insolent, disdainful
Cluster Title _____ 5. taciturn, terse, laconic, pithy, quiescent

SENTENCE COMPLETIONS

Read the sentence through carefully. Then from the five vocabulary words given in parentheses, circle the word that fits *best*.

1. Sitting alone and speaking to no one, the woman was an example of _____.
   (turpitude, reticence, meandering, analogy, mutiny)

2. It is _____ to think that every individual enjoys your company.
   (egregious, unkind, willful, presumptuous, critical)

3. One favorite object of the _____ is a hand-held mirror in which to gaze adoringly.
   (derivative, bizarre, grandiloquence, egoist, sailor)

4. Your _____ poetry has no chance of winning first prize in the creative writing contest.
   (vapid, haughty, idyllic, penurious, shrewd)

5. Because you have more than 150 thank-you notes to write, I recommend that you make them _____.
   (savvy, rude, meritorious, concise, swaggering)

6. Despite Hank's efforts to _____ the tension between his friends, the bitter feelings could not be _____.
   pacify...swaggered
   prattle...banal
   assuage...rambled
   mitigate...alleviated
   vapid...hackneyed

7. Tess's _____ reply contradicted her habitual, _____ self.
   placating...derivative
   lackluster...contemptuous
   laconic...voluble
   mollified...trite
   cliché...haughty

ONE DOESN'T BELONG

Three of the words in each grouping relate to each other somehow. Cross off the one word that does not belong with the others. For a challenge, write the word that does not belong on the line below, and try your best to define that word. *Note:* Some of the words have been taken from definitions or exercises that appear within the lessons.

1. pretentious   arrogant   supercilious   garrulous

   _____ means _____

2. conciliate   assuage   swagger   mollify

   _____ means _____

3. voluble   taciturn   loquacious   verbose

_____ means _____

4. allay   vapid   insipid   platitude

_____ means _____

5. concise   palliate   succinct   pithy

_____ means _____

THE CONVIVIAL CLUSTER

Words Relating to Friendly and Agreeable

> **affable amiable amicable congenial convivial cordial gregarious jocular levity**

---

affable *adj.* easy to talk to; easy to approach, friendly; kind; amiable

Affable baseball players willingly sign autographs for the fans; the unfriendly ones refuse.

It's fun to talk with Lisa because she's so **affable** and upbeat.

Don's friendly grin conveys his **affable** personality.

amiable *adj.* friendly, kind

Amiable Amy says only the kindest things about others; she doesn't understand the meaning of nasty.

Keith is patient, friendly, and kind—an altogether **amiable** person.

Miss Crabtree frowns and growls a lot. She's a little short on **amiability**.

amicable *adj.* showing goodwill; peaceable

The conflict came to an **amicable** end when the adversaries finally shook hands.

The **amicable** negotiations ended when the parties began to insult each other.

Blockbuster Video has **amicable** employees. They don't even give you a hard time when you forget to rewind the tape.

congenial *adj.* compatible; having kindred needs or tastes; sympathetic

Mr. and Mrs. Evans are a **congenial** couple. They share a passion for antiques and surfboarding.

Sherry won the Miss **Congeniality** award for being the most friendly, considerate, and affable contestant in the pageant.

What a **congenial** place this is! I always feel welcome here.

convivial *adj.* sociable, outgoing in a festive way, especially when pertaining to eating and drinking; fond of good company

A **convivial** crowd will be coming to the party; therefore, it should be fun.

Jake is a party animal, one of the most **convivial** guys I know.

Bad food and bad music put everyone in a bad mood. Let's try to make the next dance more **convivial**.

cordial *adj.* warm and friendly; amiable

With a **cordial** welcome, Harry made everyone feel glad to be at the meeting.

The **cordial** remarks of my guests convinced me that the party was a success.

I spend all day answering the same questions over and over, but I still try to be **cordial** to every customer.

gregarious *adj.* sociable, outgoing

I hope that Trudy soon emerges from her shell and becomes more **gregarious**.

As a child Timmy was quiet, but as a teenager he's **gregarious**.

The **gregarious** crowd kept the place buzzing all evening.

jocular *adj.* liking to be with people, joke around with them and have fun

Jay Leno's **jocular** personality makes him the perfect host for *The Tonight Show*.

Samantha is a funny person, but she's somber compared to her **jocular** sister.

There's nothing like a few **jocular** students to enliven a dull class.

levity *n.* lightheartedness; gaiety; carefree disposition, particularly when not appropriate

> "Cheating is a serious issue," said the exam proctor. "There's no room for **levity** in this discussion."

> There was plenty of loud laughter. In fact, you could hear the **levity** in the room from the other end of the corridor.

> A little **levity** is needed to lighten up this depressing class.

MEMORY TIPS

Use these mnemonics (memory devices) to boost your vocabulary. Make up your own memory clues for words in this lesson that are personally challenging. Add these two tips—and your own—to your Vocabulary Notebook. Remember, a bigger vocabulary typically means a bigger SAT I score.

amicus In Latin, **amicus** means "friend." See how the stem of this Latin word appears in several words relating to friendly: **amiable**, **amicable**. *Ami-* also appears in **amity**, which means "friendship." Consider these SAT I antonyms: **amity** ↔ **enmity**.

gregarious Learning the root word is key to remembering this word. As a Latin root, "gregis" means *herd* or *group*. Someone **gregarious** likes to be around herds of people or groups; therefore, **gregarious** means sociable.

How about this memory clue: Think **Gregarious Greg** from *The Brady Bunch*. After all, the Greg we all know and love had a big family and lots of friends!

jocular Simply, let *joc* remind you of *joking*. Now picture someone joking around, being friendly, and having fun—the personification of **jocular**! Or, try this: Picture a **jocular** jock, laughing and smiling while effortlessly twirling a basketball on his middle finger!

levity Contradictions and opposites tend to stick in our memory. So, if you know that *gravity* means "seriousness," remember its antithesis, or opposite, **levity**. Here's the visual: **levity** ↔ **gravity**.

Remember, the best memory clues are the ones that work for you.

MATCHING

Match the vocabulary words in Column A with *one or more* of their defining characteristics appearing in Column B.

Column A

a 1. affable

d 2. jocular

b 3. gregarious

c 4. levity

e 5. convivial

Column B

a. kind and friendly

b. extroverted

c. lightheartedness, humor

d. liking to joke around, have fun

e. enjoying food and good company

SAT I-STYLE ANALOGIES

First, express a clear and concise relationship between the two given terms. Next, select the pair in the answer choices that *most closely* shares a similar relationship.

1. CONVIVIAL : INTROVERTED
   a. fertile : productive
   b. undermine : strengthen
   c. unbridle : untie
   d. burgeon : fluster
   e. conduct : persuade

2. AMIABLE : CRONY
   a. strong : plaintiff
   b. demanding : heckler
   c. stringent : instructor
   d. impassive : stoic
   e. abandoned : stowaway

3. GREGARIOUS : PARTY ANIMAL
   a. subversive : religious convert
   b. typical : old tourist
   c. two-sided : loud bigot
   d. repetitive : grim storyteller
   e. fledgling : young trainee

4. GRAVITY : LEVITY
   a. open-minded : philistine
   b. phonetic : coded
   c. unilateral : multisided
   d. pug-nosed : uplifted
   e. riveting : short

5. JESTER : JOCULAR
   a. athlete : heroic
   b. pariah : triumphant
   c. scoundrel : crooked
   d. soothsayer : kindred
   e. maverick : illusionary

WORDS IN CONTEXT

Based on the context in which each **bold** word is used, identify the word usage of each sentence as either C (Correct) or I (Incorrect).

1. Gregarious Gus enjoys, above all else, the peace and calm of being alone.

2. Hilda's steady nodding showed her cordial acceptance of our change of plans.

3. Jocularity abounds during the holidays, with all the fun and festivity.

4. Saying "Please" and "Thank you" is a poor example of cordial behavior.

5. Many neighbors avoid the elderly woman due to her affable personality.

THE CANTANKEROUS CLUSTER

Words Relating to Quarreling, Fighting, and Bitter Feelings

animosity antagonism bellicose belligerent cantankerous captious contentious disputatious polemical predator pugnacious

animosity *n.* hatred; ill will

So much **animosity** grew between Mark and Mike that they never were buddies again.

Ursula's **animosity** toward Eddie hardened her heart.

Sonya's sarcasm raised the level of **animosity** between Liz and her.

antagonism *n.* hatred or hostility

Stan's mocking and teasing incited **antagonism** among his teammates.

He is tormented by the **antagonism** of his classmates, who ride him unmercifully.

Roy and Charlie used to be pals, but an argument over Millie turned them into **antagonists**.

bellicose *adj.* of a quarrelsome nature; eager to fight; warlike; belligerent

The speech was full of **bellicose** threats, suggesting war was at hand.

The **bellicose** coach lost his job after he told his players: "Kill them bums!"

After Richie's nose was broken in a fight, his **bellicose** behavior diminished.

belligerent *adj.* taking part in war or fighting; ready to fight

After two decades of war, the **belligerent** countries made peace.

When told to rewrite her essay, Gertie grew **belligerent** and yelled at her teacher.

Noah's **belligerence** started the fight.

cantankerous *adj.* bad-tempered; quarrelsome

Cantankerous Timmy is my two-year old brother. He whines a lot and throws his oatmeal all over the kitchen.

Grandma and Grandpa are a **cantankerous** old couple, always fighting and scolding.

When my dad gets up on the wrong side of the bed, he's **cantankerous** the whole day.

captious *adj.* made for the sake of quarreling; quibbling

My English teacher, Ms. Carr, quibbles over every word. She criticizes her students' writing with **captious** comments.

Jon used to be laid-back and easygoing, but since his parents' divorce he's **captious** about everything.

My supervisor does nothing but bicker with the staff. His **captiousness** forced me to quit my job.

contentious *adj.* quarrelsome; belligerent

You can't talk to **contentious** Cal without getting into an argument.

I get along well with my sister, but my brother and I are usually **contentious**.

If you don't stop being **contentious**, no one will want to cooperate with you.

disputatious *adj.* likely to dispute or argue

Ken loves to argue just for the sake of arguing. With such a **disputatious** personality, he's sure to be a trial lawyer.

I don't want to be **disputatious**, but I think you are completely wrong about Hester's motives.

Hoping to provoke lively class discussions, Mr. Phillips raises controversial issues and assumes a **disputatious** personality.

polemical *adj.* inclined to argue or debate; controversial

When Donna disagrees, she doesn't calmly differ with you, but tends to be **polemical**.

Because their feelings ran high, several senators engaged in strong **polemical** exchanges to support their opinions.

The speech was not a reasonable argument against gun control; it was more of a **polemic**.

predator *n.* one who takes advantage of another, exploits or feeds on another; a strong adversary or rival

Tonight I'll try to catch the **predator** who raided the henhouse last night and killed my prize rooster.

He's a con man, a known **predator** on unsuspecting old folks who trust him to profitably invest their life savings.

Watch out for **predatory** schemers who'll take your money and run.

pugnacious *adj.* eager to fight; belligerent

Pugnacious Paul, as you might expect, was involved in another schoolyard brawl.

Walter and Willa are a **pugnacious** pair, always squabbling and fighting.

Beware of **pugnacious** salesmen who'll bully you into buying things you don't need.

MEMORY TIPS

Use these mnemonics (memory devices) to boost your vocabulary. Make up your own memory clues for words in this lesson that are personally challenging. Add these catchy tips—and your own—to your Vocabulary Notebook. Remember, vocabulary building is key to increasing your score on the verbal SAT I.

antagonism From your English class discussions, you most likely already know who an *antagonist* is. He or she is the person who rivals the novel's main character, or protagonist. Since these two characters are in opposition, there is a feeling of **antagonism** between them. Now, simply put, remember that a story's antagonist is likely to feel a sense of **antagonism** (hostility, aversion) toward the rival protagonist.

bellicose, belligerent "Belli" is a Latin root for war. By memorizing this word root, you can help yourself learn two words for the price of one root!

cantankerous Have you ever had a canker sore in your mouth? If so, you know how uncomfortable, even painful, one can be. If Casey had a canker sore in his mouth, then he might be **cantankerous** (bad-tempered, quarrelsome). Think of "canker sore" when you see **cantankerous.**

pugnacious Remember the schoolyard bully? Create a picture in your mind's eye of the bully as *pug*-nosed and ruddy-faced. Can you see the bully? Now, link *pug* from pug-nosed to the *pug* in the vocabulary word **pugnacious** (ready to fight).

MATCHING

Match the vocabulary words in Column A with *one or more* of their defining characteristics appearing in Column B.

Column A	Column B
1. polemical b,d	a. ready to fight
2. contentious e	b. liking to argue
3. predator c	c. one who takes advantage of others
4. disputatious b	d. controversial
5. belligerent a	e. bad-tempered

SAT I-STYLE ANALOGIES

First, express a clear and concise relationship between the two given terms. Next, select the pair in the answer choices that *most closely* shares a similar relationship.

1. CONTENTIOUS : AGREEABLE

    a. meager : abundant
    b. believable : indecipherable
    c. yearning : begging
    d. content : glad
    e. toting : even

2. MANNERS : PREDATORY

    a. jitters : calm
    b. nuances : humdrum
    c. trivets : orderly
    d. victories : inquisitive
    e. pitfalls : laggardly

3. POLEMICAL : DEBATE

    a. rapturous : trinkets
    b. quizzical : maxims
    c. lucid : mantras
    d. nocturnal : vapor
    e. erudite : learning

4. ANTAGONISTIC : PEACE-MAKING

    a. munificent : skimping
    b. pedantic : pelting
    c. athletic : kicking
    d. magnanimous : giving
    e. jaded : coloring

5. WRANGLER : DISPUTATIOUS

    a. bumpkin : rustic
    b. contender : elitist
    c. brigand : celestial
    d. student : ambivalent
    e. practitioner : innovative

WORDS IN CONTEXT

Based on the context in which each **bold** word is used, identify the word usage of each sentence as either C (Correct) or I (Incorrect).

1. Dean White's antagonistic remarks inspired gratitude and warmth in the student body of Caliope High.

2. However content one may be, one is likely to become contentious every once in a while.

3. Pugnacious tendencies aside, Leo was best characterized as tolerant and agreeable.

4. Complaining shrilly and demanding more than was deserved, the irritable IHOP patron behaved antagonistically.

5. Patty and Pete are predatory partners; they accommodate each other's needs so that each benefits from a feeling of well-being.

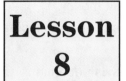

THE GIVING GROUP

Words Relating to Generosity in Spending Money or Time, or Showing Concern for Others

Lesson 8

altruistic benevolent largess lavish magnanimous munificent philanthropic prodigal squander

---

altruistic *adj.* showing an unselfish concern for others

Donna is a supreme example of **altruism**. She leads youth groups, delivers meals to the homebound, and volunteers at the local hospital.

Altruistic Al never thinks of himself; he devotes all his time to helping others.

Barbara's motives were not altogether **altruistic**. She had much to gain from serving as the head of the school's blood drive.

benevolent *adj.* giving freely and easily to others; charitable; kind

Ready to help anyone at any time, Tina is about the most **benevolent** person I know.

A **benevolent** streak in Dr. Little compelled him to give up his lucrative practice in New York and help fight AIDS in Africa.

No one has helped our library as much as you have. Your **benevolence** is greatly appreciated.

largess *n.* generous giving

Sam is famous for his **largess**. Knowing Sam is a big tipper, the staff at his favorite hotel is always glad to see him.

To survive on the street, beggars often depend on the **largess** of passersby.

The **largess** of their alumni has enabled many colleges to offer scholarships to deserving students.

lavish *adj.* generous in giving to others or in spending money

For her sixteenth birthday, Sarah received **lavish** gifts, including a trip to Hawaii and a BMW convertible.

Despite a modest income, the McTaveys make **lavish** donations to their church.

Because Rod spent **lavishly** on scuba diving gear and hot-air ballooning, he couldn't afford to pay his phone bill.

magnanimous *adj.* generous in overlooking insult or injury by others; rising above pettiness

After the attempt on his life, the Pope **magnanimously** forgave the man who shot him.

It's amazing that a man as selfish as James has the nerve to call himself **magnanimous**.

Mr. Appel **magnanimously** offered full college scholarships to any children in the sixth grade who stayed in school and graduated from high school.

munificent *adj.* very generous

It's easy to be **munificent** when you already have more of everything than you'll ever want or need.

In a **munificent** act of friendship, Eileen gave up her tickets to the concert so that Emily could go with her new boyfriend.

Her **munificence** was evident in the costly gifts she gave to her family and friends.

philanthropic *adj.* showing a desire to help others by giving gifts; charitable; humane

My mother works for a **philanthropic** organization that disburses funds to needy hospitals.

Bill Gates donates millions of dollars a year to education, medical research, and other **philanthropic** causes.

By definition, a **philanthropist** helps those in need.

prodigal *adj.* wasteful; lavish

Marcia's **prodigal** spending at the mall used up the money she'd been saving for college. Next time, maybe she'll spend more thoughtfully.

Unable to control his expenses, Krups spent **prodigally** until he was broke.

The maxim "A penny saved is a penny earned" means nothing to **prodigal**s like Hillary and Hal.

squander *vb.* to spend money (or time) in a wasteful, uncaring fashion

Jimmy **squandered** a perfectly good day aimlessly watching TV from dawn to dusk.

"Don't **squander** your paycheck on designer clothes" advised Aunt Rose. "Spend it on something useful."

Because he wasn't thinking straight at the time, Roy **squandered** his chance for a great summer job in Washington.

MEMORY TIPS

Use these mnemonics (memory devices) to boost your vocabulary. Make up your own memory clues for words in this lesson that are personally challenging. Add these two tips—and your own—to your Vocabulary Notebook. Remember, vocabulary building is key to increasing your score on the verbal SAT I.

benevolent As a frequently used prefix, *bene-* means *good.* Remember that simple word root, and the sense of *good-willing* will come through when you see the word **benevolent.** Additional words that start with the prefix *bene-* include: benediction (a blessing), benefactor (a do-gooder), and beneficial (helpful).

largess If you're a visual learner (most of us are), this memory tip will appeal to you. Because **largess** means generous giving, let this word picture work for you: **LARGE$$**. Each S becomes a dollar sign to symbolize the giving nature of this word. "*Large* giving," or **largess**, does not have to exclusively mean giving money. Largess can also deal with giving your time or giving gifts.

magnanimous Once again, word roots are your memory clue. "Magna" means *big*, and "animus" means *spirit*. Link these two roots together, and you get *big-spirited*, the sense of generosity behind **magnanimous.**

MATCHING

Match the vocabulary words in Column A with *one or more* of their defining characteristics appearing in Column B.

Column A	Column B
1. lavish a	a. big-spirited when it comes to giving
2. prodigal e	b. to spend too freely
3. squander b	c. showing concern for others
4. altruistic c	d. good willing
5. benevolent c+d	e. wasteful

SAT I-STYLE ANALOGIES

First, express a clear and concise relationship between the two given terms. Next, select the pair in the answer choices that *most closely* shares a similar relationship.

1. PHILANTHROPIST : ALTRUISTIC
   a. acrobat : prodigious
   b. carpenter : jaunty
   c. corpse : lifeless
   d. prankster : venomous
   e. competitor : cowardly

2. MAGNANIMOUS : MUNIFICENT
   a. friendly : laggardly
   b. hyper : moody
   c. yearning : bendable
   d. coy : crabby
   e. merciless : ruthless

3. PRODIGAL : WASTREL
   a. curvaceous : woman
   b. angel-like : cherub
   c. ungrateful : minstrel
   d. defensive : constituent
   e. cranial : principal

4. PENNY-PINCHING : LAVISH
   a. teeth-clenching : easeful
   b. breath-holding : attentive
   c. nail-biting : disdainful
   d. feet-stomping : musical
   e. body-swaying : mindful

5. BENEVOLENT : BENEDICTION
   a. helpful : profanity
   b. incisive : remark
   c. keen : formula
   d. kind : compliment
   e. healthy : grace

WORDS IN CONTEXT

Based on the context in which each **bold** word is used, identify the word usage of each sentence as either C (Correct) or I (Incorrect).

1. In order to teach her nephew how to squander his nickels and pennies, Aunt Laura bought Trevor a blue piggy bank.

2. Receiving gifts is Jane's delight, for hers is an altruistic soul.

3. Benevolent gestures are meant to better the lives of others.

4. Respected for her consistent magnanimity, Dina was recognized as "Do-Gooder of the Year."

5. Prodigal spending habits are unlikely to pay off in the long run.

<table>
<tr><td>

Lesson 9

</td><td>

PENNY-PINCHING TIGHTWAD?

Words Relating to Cheapness or Care with Spending Money

</td></tr>
</table>

austere avarice frugal mercenary miserly parsimonious
penurious thrifty

---

austere *adj.* having great economy; showing self-control when it comes to foregoing luxuries, frills; stern in manner or appearance

The poet had lived an **austere** life, foregoing all luxuries and creature comforts.

Early in their marriage, my parents lived on an **austere** budget that allowed them to buy nothing beyond the bare essentials.

To save money on our trip, we stayed in **austere** little motels that provided little more than a bed and a shower.

avarice *n.* greed

The mayor's **avarice** caused him to embezzle funds from the city's coffers.

She was young and beautiful; he was old but very rich. Rumors said that **avarice** drove her to marry him.

Avarice motivates many people to cheat on their income tax.

frugal *adj.* careful with money; thrifty; not costly

As a **frugal** carpenter, Emil finds a use for every scrap of wood. Nothing goes to waste in Emil's shop.

Surprisingly, they were **frugal** at breakfast, but they spared no expense at dinner.

Frugality kept the old woman from spending a penny on anything she didn't absolutely need.

mercenary *adj.* greedy for self-gain; thinking only of money-making

The **mercenary** owner of the leather store was too money-hungry to ever hold a sale.

He cared little about the quality of his merchandise. As a **mercenary**, he focused only on the size of his profit.

What appeared at first to be **mercenary**, turned out to be a totally unselfish endeavor.

miserly *adj.* careful with how money is spent; thrifty

To lose weight, I eat a **miserly** breakfast: one prune and a cup of fat-free milk.

Too **miserly** to spend a dollar, she'd rather walk than take the cross-town bus.

I never realized what a **miser** Eric was until he refused to give me a sip from his water bottle when we were hiking together.

parsimonious *adj.* overly thrifty or miserly

Gramps is **parsimonious** with his words. Sometimes he doesn't speak for days.

Parsimonious Paul never buys anything unless it's on sale.

He's generous to his family, but to outsiders he is the epitome of **parsimony**.

penurious *adj.* stingy; relating to great poverty, destitution

His **penurious** childhood taught my father the value of every penny.

Stop being so **penurious** and give a few dollars to help the homeless.

The **penury** of the family was made apparent by the small cup of soup and crust of bread that Ma served for dinner.

thrifty *adj.* showing care with how money and resources are spent or used; miserly

Being **thrifty** is one thing, but being downright cheap is another.

Be **thrifty** for the next few months, and you'll save enough for a new stereo.

Mama practiced **thrift** by dressing the kids in hand-me-downs rather than in new clothes.

MEMORY TIPS

Use these mnemonics (memory devices) to boost your vocabulary. Make up your own memory clues for words in this lesson that are personally challenging. Add these two tips—and your own—to your Vocabulary Notebook. Remember, vocabulary building is key to increasing your score on the verbal SAT I.

au<u>ster</u>e Link the letter cluster *ster* to the *ster* in <u>ster</u>n. Also, let "severe," which is a synonym for this vocabulary word, be a rhyming definition for **austere**. The noun form is **austerity**. You can link austerity to severity as a rhyming, synonym pair. Think in terms of severity/austerity when it comes to cutting back on spending, for example.

<u>me</u>rcenary Think *me!* when you see this word. One who is **mercenary** thinks primarily of self-gain (*me!*). In your Vocabulary Notebook, write MErcenary with a highlighted, capital ME to emphasize this clue for *greedy*.

par<u>simoni</u>ous How this word sounds is key to this mnemonic. Think of someone taking *moni* (money) and putting it in her *pars* (purse). See this simple act as a symbol of cheapness, the basic meaning of **parsimonious**.

penurious Because "penniless" sounds similar to **penurious**, let "penniless" be a simple, rhyming definition for this word. The noun form of this word, **penury**, means "poverty." **Penury** (*n.*) and "poverty" also sound alike, don't they? They both have three syllables, and they start and end with the same letters, p.....y.

thrifty Unlike miserly, **thrifty** has a positive connotation. To remind you that it's often beneficial to be **thrifty**, use this rhyming chant: "It's nifty to be **thrifty**! It's nifty to be **thrifty**! It's nifty to be **thrifty**!" Repeat this chant three times. **Thrift** is the noun form.

MATCHING

Match the vocabulary words in Column A with *one or more* of their defining characteristics appearing in Column B.

Column A	Column B
1. austere	a. one who hoards money for himself
2. avarice	b. economizing
3. penurious	c. penniless
4. frugal	d. greed
5. miser	e. restricted with spending

SAT I-STYLE ANALOGIES

First, express a clear and concise relationship between the two given terms. Next, select the pair in the answer choices that *most closely* shares a similar relationship.

1. PENURIOUS : EXTRAVAGANT

 a. humorous : frugal
 b. stubborn : yielding
 c. taciturn : morose
 d. slanted : pliable
 e. vague : concentric

2. MISER : AUSTERE

 a. renegade : disloyal
 b. heretic : displaced
 c. investor : relentless
 d. stoic : shy
 e. tour guide : understanding

3. MERCENARY: OPENHEARTED

 a. hidden : hermetic
 b. gleeful : mild
 c. contrite : remorseful
 d. truculent : young
 e. exotic : typical

4. BENEFACTOR : MISER

 a. violinist : conductor
 b. heathen : janitor
 c. firebrand : peacemaker
 d. ghost : philatelist
 e. demon : patriot

5. HOARDS : PARSIMONIOUS
   a. yodels : talented
   b. discerns : omnivorous
   c. discriminates : selective
   d. rescinds : determined
   e. tantalizes : tortuous

6. THRIFTY : PARSIMONIOUS
   a. gluttonous : jolly
   b. hysterical : unwitting
   c. impish : voluminous
   d. subtle : slender
   e. sweet : mawkish

WORDS IN CONTEXT

Based on the context in which each **bold** word is used, identify the word usage of each sentence as either C (Correct) or I (Incorrect).

1. "Your untidy room proves that you are miserly!" scolded older sister.

2. Parsimony portends the increasing selfishness of humankind.

3. Using a sheet of paper on only one side is a sign of a miserly individual.

4. Mercenaries and tightwads are two of a kind.

5. Dishearteningly, penurious living conditions can contribute to despair and ill will on the part of the dwellers.

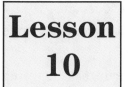

MOLE HILLS OR MOUNTAINS?

Lesson 10

Words Relating to Problems, Puzzlements, and Disasters

adversity conflagration confounding cryptic debacle enigma
labyrinth precarious quagmire quandary turbulence turmoil

---

adversity *n.* great trouble or difficulty

The book tells how he overcame the **adversity** of an impoverished childhood.

The hero faced four years of **adversity** trying to survive on a deserted island.

If you can get through junior year in high school, you can get through any **adversity** that may come along.

conflagration *n.* a huge fire, an inferno

Flames from the **conflagration** lit up the sky for miles around.

The burning of Atlanta is one of the great **conflagration** scenes in movie history.

During the **conflagration** of 1991, 3,000 homes burned to the ground.

confounding *adj.* puzzling; baffling

The world was fascinated by the **confounding** disappearance of Amelia Earhart.

Who ate the strawberries continues to be a **confounding** mystery.

The possible existence of extraterrestrial life has **confounded** scientists for centuries.

cryptic *adj.* hidden; hard to understand; mysterious; obscure

We found a **cryptic** message scrawled on the blackboard. No one could figure out its meaning.

The twins used a **cryptic**, incomprehensible language to talk with each other.

The agent left a trail of **cryptic** notes that only the spymaster could decipher.

debacle *n.* a failure or breakdown; a collapse that is often nonsensical

For me, physics class was a **debacle**. I understood none of it, failed every test, and finally dropped the course.

The 45–0 score suggests that the game was a **debacle** for the losing side.

The play was a **debacle**. Actors forgot their lines, the set fell down, and the lights blew halfway through the first act.

enigma *n.* a riddle or mystery; a puzzling or baffling matter or person

Isabelle is an **enigma**. I can't figure her out. Her moods change like the wind, and sometimes I haven't the faintest idea what she's talking about.

James acts mysteriously to prevent others from understanding him too well. He prefers to remain an **enigma**.

The **enigmatic** carvings on the ancient Egyptian tomb never have been fully interpreted.

labyrinth *n.* a maze from which it is very hard to extricate (free) oneself

The basement of our school is a **labyrinth** of tunnels, criss-crossing passageways, and dead ends in which it is easy to lose your way.

The plumbing system in my house is a **labyrinth** of copper pipes that turn and bend every which way.

Applying to college often seems like trying to find your way through a complicated maze, or **labyrinth**.

precarious *adj.* dangerous or risky; uncertain

Bungee jumping is too **precarious** for me; I prefer safer activities like playing chess.

Because Finny's foothold on the tree limb was **precarious**, he fell and broke his leg.

It's **precarious** to apply to only one college because you may not be admitted, and then what?

quagmire *n.* a difficult or troubling situation; a swampy ground, bog

A **quagmire** of troubles kept Julia awake at night.

Once Pete freed himself from his **quagmire** of unpaid bills, he began to reorganize his finances afresh.

Unable to avoid the quicksand, Rebecca began sinking into the **quagmire**!

quandary *n.* a dilemma; a confusing or puzzling situation

Walter faced the enviable **quandary** of deciding which of three hot colleges he should attend.

Confronted with the **quandary** of staying home with her new baby or going back to work, my sister chose to return to her job.

Safe Rides has taken the **quandary** out of whether to accept a ride with a driver who's been drinking.

turbulence *n.* great unrest; turmoil or disorder

In September Mac and Meg were a happy couple. Since Mary came along, their relationship has experienced some **turbulence**.

Migrating whales caused the **turbulence** in the water.

To give passengers a smooth flight, the pilot steered his plane around the air **turbulence**.

turmoil *n.* a very puzzling scenario or situation; tumult

There was **turmoil** in the room because the teacher had lost control of the class.

Gretchen's emotions were in **turmoil** after Jerry unexpectedly broke up with her.

Terry took a long walk in the peaceful woods to escape the **turmoil** in her house.

MEMORY TIPS

Use these mnemonics (memory devices) to boost your vocabulary. Make up your own memory clues for words in this lesson that are personally challenging. Add these two tips—and your own—to your Vocabulary Notebook. Remember, vocabulary building is key to increasing your score on the verbal SAT I.

As the following examples show, using your preexisting knowledge is a highly effective way to learn "new" information:

adversity As you might already know, an *adversary* is an opponent or foe. So, think of **adversity** as any situation that presents a problem or difficult situation, just as an adversary does.

cryptic Likewise, as you might already know, a *crypt* is a cave. Inside a cave, it's dark. Writing on the wall, for example, is hard to read. You can picture the inside of a cave, right? So, link your familiarity with what a cave is to this vocabulary word, **cryptic** (hidden, obscure, dark).

MATCHING

Match the vocabulary words in Column A with *one or more* of their defining characteristics appearing in Column B.

Column A	Column B
1. conflagration	a. big trouble
2. adversity	b. a very difficult situation
3. precarious	c. uncertain or risky
4. quandary	d. a huge fire
5. cryptic	e. hidden, mysterious

SAT I-STYLE ANALOGIES

First, express a clear and concise relationship between the two given terms. Next, select the pair in the answer choices that *most closely* shares a similar relationship.

1. SECRET CODE : CRYPTIC

   a. old saying : regulated
   b. dull message : engaging
   c. memoir story : personal
   d. famous speech : old
   e. family joke : restored

2. QUANDARY : BEFUDDLING

   a. quote : estimable
   b. cinch : revocable
   c. slab : soluble
   d. trinket : manageable
   e. diversion : amusing

3. FLAME : CONFLAGRATION

   a. snowball : icicle
   b. inch : meadow
   c. trench : gorge
   d. chassis : cycle
   e. bulge : dam

4. TURBULENCE : TUMULT

   a. tremor : hail
   b. load : cargo
   c. slope : mound
   d. coil : center
   e. sphere : radius

5. ADVERSITY : MISFORTUNE

   a. lesson : parable
   b. challenge : derangement
   c. danger : aid
   d. weakness : feebleness
   e. vanity : modality

WORDS IN CONTEXT

Based on the context in which each **bold** word is used, identify the word usage of each sentence as either C (Correct) or I (Incorrect).

1. **Turmoil** is the manifestation of a tranquil mind.

2. Where there is overcrowding, a **conflagration** is scarcely detectable.

3. How you manage **adversity** tells something about your inner character.

4. **Enigmatic** situations require a great deal of thinking.

5. Conflicting values and backgrounds can contribute to some degree of interpersonal **turmoil**.

NAME THAT CLUSTER

To the left of the groups of words, put the Roman numeral that corresponds with these theme (or cluster) titles:

Words Relating to . . .

I. Cheapness or Care with Spending Money
II. Friendly and Agreeable
III. Generosity in Spending Money or Time, or Showing Concern for Others
IV. Quarreling, Fighting, and Bitter Feelings
V. Problems, Puzzlements, and Disasters

Cluster Title _____ 1. benevolent, largess, munificent, philanthropic, magnanimity

Cluster Title _____ 2. amicable, amiable, cordial, gregarious, jocular

Cluster Title _____ 3. quandary, adversity, debacle, labyrinth, cryptic

Cluster Title _____ 4. bellicose, antagonistic, captious, contentious, predator

Cluster Title _____ 5. frugal, penurious, thrifty, austere, miserly

SENTENCE COMPLETIONS

Read the sentence through carefully. Then from the five vocabulary words given in parentheses, circle the word that fits *best*.

1. "Sweetheart," Mr. Dire said to his wife, "we need to go on a tight budget. In other words, we have to practice some _____ around here."
(benevolence, amity, austerity, conflagration, debacle)

2. Are you shy around unfamiliar people, or do you consider yourself _____?
(frugal, antagonistic, turbulent, parsimonious, gregarious)

3. Gwyneth is in such a (an) _____ mood. It's as if she can't wait to bite the head off the next person who opens his mouth! (prodigal, altruistic, convivial, thrifty, contentious)

4. Walking along wet, mossy stones in the water is _____; you just might slip, cut yourself, and fall headfirst into the water. (parsimonious, precarious, pugnacious, philanthropic, polemical)

5. With her balloon sculpting and bubble blowing, Cleo the Clown created an atmosphere of _____ that every guest enjoyed. (antagonism, avarice, animosity, levity, munificence)

6. Although delightfully _____ at public gatherings, enigmatic (puzzling) Lucas tends to be _____ and uptight when at home.
captious...bellicose
cryptic...altruistic
thrifty...penurious
amicable...convivial
jocular...cantankerous

7. The devastating _____ at the Jones's place of business seemed to kick off a chain reaction of negative events; one _____ followed by another.
conflagration...adversity
debacle...levity
frugality...antagonism
largess...altruism
turmoil...prodigal

ONE DOESN'T BELONG

Three of the words in each grouping relate to each other somehow. Cross off the one word that does not belong with the others. For a challenge, write the word that does not belong on the line below, and try your best to define that word. *Note:* Some of the words have been taken from definitions or exercises that appear within the lessons.

1. cantankerous   altruistic   belligerent   antagonistic

   _____ means _____

2. parsimonious   avaricious   conundrum   miserly

   _____ means _____

3. congenial   amenable   convivial   squander

   _____ means _____

4. confounding   mercenary   enigmatic   obscure

   _____ means _____

5. conflagration   magnanimous   philanthropic   charitable

   _____ means _____

THE BAD, THE VERY BAD, AND THE BADDEST

Words Relating to Harmful or Mean

baneful deleterious detrimental devious iniquitous malicious nefarious odious ominous pernicious rancorous virulent

---

baneful *adj.* causing ruin; harmful; pernicious

My campus visit was **baneful**. When it was over, I resolved never to go near the place again.

A teacher's **baneful** comments about Becky destroyed her chances of getting into the Honor Society.

Norman's **baneful** remark about Nora's hair ruined the rest of her day.

deleterious *adj.* harmful to one's health or overall welfare; pernicious

PCBs and other harmful pollutants have had a **deleterious** effect on fish in the Hudson River.

Many processed foods contain chemicals and other ingredients that can be **deleterious** to our health.

The arrogance of the new principal had a **deleterious** effect on the morale of the school's staff and students.

detrimental *adj.* harmful

To the **detriment** of its Nielsen ratings, *Friends* went on the air at the same time as *Survivor* and lost 25 percent of its audience.

Smoking is known to be **detrimental** to your health.

The trouble Steve caused had a **detrimental** effect on the class's test scores.

devious *adj.* dishonest or deceptive

The sly, **devious** fox outwitted the farmer and broke into the henhouse.

Russ is too **devious** to trust with the keys to the equipment closet.

The neighbors could not believe that someone as upright as Hanssen could have been so **devious**.

iniquitous *adj.* showing a lack of fairness; wicked; vicious

The **iniquitous** referee plainly favored the other team over ours. Every call went against our team.

Income tax cuts that benefit the wealthy will only further the **iniquitous** economic divide between the wealthy and the less fortunate.

Iniquity has no place in a courtroom dedicated to justice.

malicious *adj.* intending to hurt or harm another; spiteful

By the show's end, the heckler's insensitive remarks became downright **malicious**.

Malicious gossip did irreparable harm to Hans's reputation.

To save his own neck, Boris **maliciously** accused Beatrice of a crime she didn't commit.

nefarious *adj.* very mean and wicked

Of all the rotten scoundrels in the story, Sebastian was the most **nefarious**.

His desire to get a conviction caused the **nefarious** police officer to plant incriminating evidence at the scene of the crime.

Extortion of kids' lunch money is just one example of Hubert's **nefariousness**.

odious *adj.* loathsome; evil; revolting in a disgusting way

John has the **odious** habit of clipping his toenails in class.

I can't imagine a more **odious** crime than child abuse.

Steerforth was an **odious** character who betrayed his friends and told nothing but lies.

ominous *adj.* pertaining to an evil omen; foreboding

The dark clouds on the horizon looked **ominous**.

The settlers considered the gravestones alongside the trail **ominous** signs of hardships to come.

Superstitious people regard broken mirrors and black cats as **ominous**.

pernicious *adj.* very destructive or harmful, usually in an inconspicuous and relentless way

From the Columbine incident, Ralph got the **pernicious** idea to take a gun to school.

Lady Macbeth planted in her husband's mind the **pernicious** scheme of killing the king and seizing the crown.

Cigarette smoke caused a **pernicious** growth to form in Mr. Down's lungs. Eventually, the malignancy killed him.

rancorous *adj.* deeply hateful or spiteful; malicious

The dinner conversation turned **rancorous** when Louis and Max started to argue.

A **rancorous** feud between two families lies at the heart of *Romeo and Juliet*.

I once felt bitter about her deception, but now I've lost my **rancor**.

virulent *adj.* extremely poisonous; deadly; full of spiteful hatred

Rattlesnakes are **virulent**; their poison can be fatal.

Although the fumes seem harmless, they are extremely **virulent**.

Bubonic plague was a **virulent** disease that killed millions in medieval Europe.

MEMORY TIPS

Use these mnemonics (memory devices) to boost your vocabulary. Make up your own memory clues for words in this lesson that are personally challenging. Add these tips—and your own—to your Vocabulary Notebook. Remember, memory tips that *you* create are usually the most memorable.

deleter**ious** Imagine something so harmful that it could potentially *delete* its victim. As you can see, this mnemonic uses an existing letter cluster within this vocabulary word.

malic**ious** The prefix *mal-* (meaning *bad*) is helpful to know. Additional SAT I words containing this prefix include malevolent (bad-willed), malefactor (an evildoer), and malign (to bad-mouth, slander).

nefarious Do you remember Jefar from the Disney movie *Aladdin*? Jefar was one mean character. Link Jefar to *nefar***ious**.

ominous Did you know that an *omen* is a sign of something to come in the future—a prophetic sign? (For example, a black cat is an omen for bad luck; a dark cloud is an omen for rainy weather or forthcoming doom.) Well, if you know the word *omen,* you can see how the adjective **ominous** is derived from this simpler word.

Note: Omens can be good or bad. Something **ominous**, however, relates only to something bad.

virul**ent** This chant might help: "**Virulent** virus! **Virulent** virus! **Virulent** virus!" Your preexisting knowledge tells you that a virus is something harmful; simply link that to the meaning of **virulent**.

MATCHING

Match the vocabulary words in Column A with *one or more* of their defining characteristics appearing in Column B.

Column A

1. virulent a
2. rancorous c
3. nefarious d
4. pernicious e
5. ominous b

Column B

a. potentially deadly
b. portending doom
c. filled with bitter ill will
d. sinister
e. very harmful

SAT I-STYLE ANALOGIES

First, express a clear and concise relationship between the two given terms. Next, select the pair in the answer choices that *most closely* shares a similar relationship.

1. DELETERIOUS : TOXIN
   a. heartfelt : message
   b. simple : life
   c. rhythmic : song
   d. gracious : lily
   e. lively : tremor

2. PROSPEROUS : BANEFUL
   a. healthy : huge
   b. yielding : submissive
   c. attentive : aloof
   d. grand : slim
   e. notorious : legal

3. DEVIOUS : ABOVEBOARD
   a. broad : narrow
   b. vague : undefined
   c. bland : blissful
   d. natural : illusory
   e. elusive : euphoric

4. ODIOUS : MURDER
   a. typical : coaching
   b. wily : junket
   c. layered : skiing
   d. illusory : magic
   e. geriatric : age

5. VILLAIN : NEFARIOUS
   a. gargoyle : light-hearted
   b. craftsman : tricky
   c. deacon : elegant
   d. expert : dogmatic
   e. dynamo : vivacious

WORDS IN CONTEXT

Based on the context in which each **bold** word is used, identify the word usage of each sentence as either C (Correct) or I (Incorrect).

C 1. The virulent vapors produced headaches and nausea in those who breathed them in.

I 2. Rancor is born from friendships that have lasted too long.

C 3. Sneaking out of the house at night and making up stories about post-curfew whereabouts are examples of devious conduct.

C 4. The fictitious character's nefarious ways made him the perfect antagonist to the kindly police officer.

I 5. Filled with anxiety, the young apprentice felt at ease when he saw the ominous visions.

Lesson 12

YOU SHOULD NOT HAVE DONE THAT!

Words Relating to Criticizing, Disapproving, or Scolding

berate carp castigate censure chastise deprecate deride
impugn rebuff rebuke reprove upbraid

berate *vb.* to rebuke or scold in a harsh tone

Her parents often **berated** her, but when the scoldings took place in front of her friends, Lulu was humiliated.

The teacher **berated** Jonathan for shouting an obscenity in class.

I don't like to **berate** my children, but this is the last straw. If you come home late again, you can expect a good scolding.

carp *vb.* to find fault; to be critical

"**Carping** won't get you anywhere," said the teacher to the nit-picking child. "But expressing your problem-solving ideas will be beneficial to the entire class."

To **carp** is to harp on your discontentment without taking any positive steps toward improving your circumstance.

Sullen and ill-tempered, the **carping** carp stewed at the bottom of the lake, complaining about the cold water, the slimy eels, and the lack of tasty food. (See Memory Tip.)

castigate *vb.* to scold or punish severely

Before **castigating** others about speeding, ask yourself if you always obey the speed limit.

Fearing **castigation**, Myron made sure that he handed in his lab report on time.

The policeman not only issued him a ticket, but **castigated** him for 10 minutes about passing a stopped school bus.

censure *vb.* to criticize strongly

> A letter of **censure**, criticizing his behavior, was put in his file.

> For harassing his secretary, Mr. Packwood was **censured**, but not fired, from his job.

> After being publicly **censured**, the woman vowed never to shoplift again.

chastise *vb.* to punish or scold harshly

> My parents **chastised** me for putting bubble gum in my little sister's hair.

> Being grounded for a month is the worst **chastisement** Loren ever got.

> I accept my **chastisement**. It was stupid of me to drive the car across the golf course.

deprecate *vb.* to show mild disapproval

> In class we make only positive comments. Remarks that **deprecate** the work of others are prohibited.

> Although I tried very hard this semester, Ms. Bluestone **deprecated** my efforts to improve.

> They respond only to praise. **Deprecation** doesn't change their behavior at all.

deride *vb.* to ridicule or make fun of; to scoff at

> Do you think that **deriding** others will make you look better? It won't!

> Ironically, the same critic who **derided** the play last year praised it this year.

> Filled with **derision**, the cocky young man made fun of one person after another.

impugn *vb.* to oppose or attack someone or something as false or refutable

> The scandal **impugned** the reputation of the judge.

> Don't **impugn** my honesty. I never stole a library book.

No one subscribes to that theory anymore. It was **impugned** by new research.

rebuff *vb.* to snub; to bluntly refuse

Gigi **rebuffed** Dick's proposal, so Dick asked Margie instead.

Grant's initial request for a raise was **rebuffed**, but he got an increase the second time he asked.

I hoped to make up with him after the argument, but I was **rebuffed**.

rebuke *vb.* to reprimand or scold sharply

Jill **rebuked** Jack for breaking his crown. "I promise not to do it again," said Jack.

Sarah continued to bite her nails in spite of being **rebuked** time and again.

Charlie won't **rebuke** me for deceiving him. He understands and given the chance would probably do the same to me.

reprove *vb.* to speak to in a disapproving manner; to scold

Reprovingly, the teacher said, "For the last time, I'm telling you that absence is no excuse for not doing the work."

The teacher **reproved** Sonny for not bringing a note from his parents.

"Stop it!" shouted Mike, "I won't have you **reprove** me for an offense I didn't commit."

upbraid *vb.* to chide; to scold bitterly

Mr. Judd **upbraided** the class for throwing pencils and paper clips around the room.

I hate to be scolded for missing a deadline. I should be **upbraided** for many worse things.

Janet **upbraided** her sister for eavesdropping on her phone calls. "Stay out of my love life," she chided.

MEMORY TIPS

Use these mnemonics (memory devices) to boost your vocabulary. Make up your own memory clues for words in this lesson that are challenging for you. Add these two tips—and your own—to your Vocabulary Notebook.

carp Do you know what a carp is? That's right—a freshwater fish! Let's link carp to **carping** by imagining a "carping carp" swimming in a lake. Picture this carp in your mind's eye. What could he be **carping** about—the cloudy water? Too many fish in the pond? Not enough food? Water pollution? Who knows? Picture this carp complaining about and being critical about so many things. He is indeed a "***carping** carp.*"

deprecate Do you know what it means for a car (or any asset) to depreciate in value? It means to go down in value. So, link this understanding to **deprecate**. If someone deprecates another's idea, then that person is looking upon the idea with mild disapproval, or *a sense of lesser value*. If this connection works for you, then **deprecate** will no longer be an unknown word for you.

deride Let the letter cluster *rid* kindle *rid*icule, the meaning of this vocabulary word. To **deride** is to ridicule, mock, or make fun of.

impugn Recall *pugn* at the beginning of pugnacious (ready to fight; quarrelsome). Now, link that *pugn* meaning to the verb **impugn**. To impugn is *to oppose* or *attack*; now I'm sure you see the link between this verb and the adjective *pugnacious*. This mnemonic strategy enforces two words simultaneously.

rebuff, rebuke, reprove Let the *re* at their beginnings link them together in your mind's eye so that you can efficiently learn these three as a group. Learning this trio simultaneously will accelerate your vocabulary building.

MATCHING

Match the vocabulary words in Column A with *one or more* of their defining characteristics appearing in Column B.

Column A

1. deprecate c

2. impugn b

3. rebuff d

4. castigate e

5. berate a

Column B

a. to criticize harshly

b. to verbally attack

c. to speak to disapprovingly

d. to snub

e. to scold severely

SAT I-STYLE ANALOGIES

First, express a clear and concise relationship between the two given terms. Next, select the pair in the answer choices that *most closely* shares a similar relationship.

1. UPBRAID : EXTOL
   a. criticize : poll
   b. scorn : hail
   c. loathe : lope
   d. hinder : stampede
   e. pose : oppose

2. APPROVING : DEPRECATING
   a. gross : thoughtful
   b. flimsy : undecodable
   c. pompous : conceited
   d. giddy : serious
   e. brawny : exasperating

3. CRITICIZE : CENSURE
   a. gorge : enfold
   b. hurtle : jump
   c. swell : distend
   d. stray : evade
   e. wipe : scrub

4. CASTIGATE : CHASTISE
   a. unbridle : overturn
   b. undermine : weaken
   c. offend : levitate
   d. replete : send
   e. moan : cluck

5. IRREFUTABLE : IMPUGNED
   a. lucid : expressed
   b. feared : abhorred
   c. wild : undersized
   d. blameless : categorized
   e. amorphous : shaped

WORDS IN CONTEXT

Based on the context in which each **bold** word is used, identify the word usage of each sentence as either C (Correct) or I (Incorrect).

1. After being rebuffed by her peers, Harriet felt reassured.

2. The upbraiding lifted the spirits of all who were present.

3. The parents eyed their child deprecatingly, hoping that their displeasure would persuade the child to change.

4. The center's mission statement was impugned as unfair and narrow-minded.

5. The elder's reproving tone improved the morale of the hard-working group.

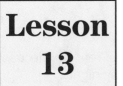

Lesson 13

WHO CARES? WHAT'S SO INTERESTING?

Words Relating to Lacking Interest or Emotion

aloof apathetic detached impassive indifferent listless
nonchalant phlegmatic remote stolid

---

aloof *adj.* uninterested; showing no concern; emotionally removed or distant

He appears to be **aloof**, but his detachment comes from shyness, not conceit.

The Parkers prefer to stay **aloof** from their neighbors. They didn't even attend the Labor Day block party.

Biff's recent **aloofness** contrasts sharply with his usual gregariousness.

apathetic *adj.* indifferent; showing no care, interest, or concern; lacking emotion

The crowd was mostly **apathetic**. They didn't give a hoot who won the game.

"I've heard this school is a hotbed of **apathy**," said the new principal. "Well, I intend to raise school spirit and make kids want to come here each day."

Because of student **apathy**, no one cared enough to collect money to help earthquake victims in India.

detached *adj.* aloof; indifferent

Jane is **detached** from class activities. She sits passively and never participates in discussions.

Ken seemed to rise above the petty bickering, but he wasn't as **detached** as he appeared.

I'm not getting involved in critiquing the play. I'm just a **detached** observer.

impassive *adj.* lacking emotion or drive

> Jake's **impassive** nature contrasts with Jenny's innate enthusiasm.

> Johnny maintained an **impassive** attitude as the rest of the cast complained about the extra rehearsal on Saturday night.

> Ten witnesses stood by with **impassive** expressions and did nothing as the killer tormented his victim.

indifferent *adj.* apathetic; showing little or no concern or care

> Vickie is an **indifferent** student. She doesn't study much and doesn't care about her mediocre grades.

> I don't want to sound **indifferent**, but it's all the same to me whether I go to college or not.

> Your **indifference** really bothers me. I wish you could get excited about the campus visit.

listless *adj.* lacking interest in something, usually because of illness, fatigue, or general sadness; spiritless

> The heat wave left me **listless**. I just couldn't get up enough energy to study physics.

> After discussing the issue, Sheila replied **listlessly**, "Whatever."

> She made a **listless** effort to enter the conversation, but she soon gave up.

nonchalant *adj.* casual and indifferent; not showing any great concern or worry about anything

> She appears to be **nonchalant** on the court, but she's really trying very hard.

> "Completing your application on time is serious business," insisted the counselor. "You mustn't be **nonchalant** about it."

> Mark wanted to follow the rules to the letter, but Monica was more **nonchalant** about them.

phlegmatic *adj.* hard to get excited or emotional; calm; slow-moving

> I feel too **phlegmatic** to go on a bike ride today. Maybe tomorrow I'll be more motivated.

Andrea is too **phlegmatic** to scream and shout about anything.

Although the coach gave the team a pep talk, they played a **phlegmatic** game.

remote *adj.* emotionally distant and disinterested; aloof; uninvolved; distant, far away

Jerry became increasingly **remote** after his parents' divorce. He stopped socializing at school and never returned my phone calls.

Our old cat had a **remote** attitude toward the new kitten, refusing to accept it as part of our household.

In *Cast Away*, the hero found himself alone on a **remote** island for four years.

stolid *adj.* lacking emotion or not showing any emotion; stoical

Carrie accepted her fate in **stolid** silence. Whatever emotions she felt remained hidden.

Girls can cry as much as they want. Boys, on the other hand, are supposed to be **stolid**.

Despite the loss of their home in the fire, the Wilsons carried on with **stolid** determination.

MEMORY TIPS

Use these mnemonics (memory devices) to boost your vocabulary. Make up your own memory clues for words in this lesson that are personally challenging. Add these tips—and your own—to your Vocabulary Notebook.

apathetic As a prefix, *a-* means *without.* "Pathos," as a root word, means *feeling.* Link this prefix and root together, and you've got *without feeling,* a workable springboard definition for **apathetic**.

impassive As a prefix, *im-* can mean *not.* Let *pass* remind you of *passion.* Putting this prefix and root together, you'll see how **impassive** means, more or less, "not having passion or interest" in something.

listless For this word, simply think *lifeless.*

MATCHING

Match the vocabulary words in Column A with *one or more* of their defining characteristics appearing in Column B.

Column A	Column B
1. remote b	a. showing no interest
2. apathetic a, c	b. distant
3. detached b	c. lacking feeling about something
4. aloof e	d. casually unconcerned
5. nonchalant d	e. unconcerned

SAT I-STYLE ANALOGIES

First, express a clear and concise relationship between the two given terms. Next, select the pair in the answer choices that *most closely* shares a similar relationship.

1. ENGAGED : ALOOF
   a. strapped : shackled
   b. hindered : aided
   c. obliged : honored
   d. trained : loosened
   e. veered : lionized

2. ZEALOT : INDIFFERENT
   a. copywriter : sensible
   b. renegade : pompous
   c. guru : uninformed
   d. aide : hyperactive
   e. fiend : ghoulish

3. EMOTIONAL : STOLID
   a. brave : craven
   b. dull : ruddy
   c. ideal : loving
   d. sullen : miserly
   e. limp : lunging

4. DETACHED : BYSTANDER
   a. urbane : politician
   b. ready : onlooker
   c. pious : friar
   d. reverent : principal
   e. nocturnal : vagabond

5. LISTLESS : LIVELY
   a. haughty : late
   b. dreary : blue
   c. poetic : visionary
   d. dreamy : romantic
   e. malleable : firm

WORDS IN CONTEXT

Based on the context in which each **bold** word is used, identify the word usage of each sentence as either C (Correct) or I (Incorrect).

1. **Impassively**, the science teacher ranted and raved when he learned that the field trip fund was cut by 35 percent.

2. The families were **indifferent** to their weekend vacation; they would have been happy with either going skiing or going outlet shopping.

3. **Nonchalance** about the suffering of humanity is commendable.

4. The annual gathering of his college fraternity was of little interest to Sam; he remained **detached** from the brotherhood.

5. Family values are extremely important. How could one be **aloof** when discussing this topic?

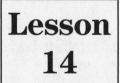

Lesson 14

NO GET UP AND GO!
Words Relating to Lacking Energy or Movement

indolent languor lassitude lethargic sedentary sluggish soporific stagnant torpid

---

indolent *adj.* lazy; not wanting to do any work

"The Lazy Boy" is a perfect title for a story about an **indolent** youth.

Indolence kept Alicia from finishing the assignment. I hope she won't be so lazy in the future.

Kevin deserves a reputation for **indolence**. He spends more time taking breaks than doing the work.

languor *n.* a weak or lifeless feeling

By nine o'clock I feel too **languorous** to do anything except watch TV.

To prevent **languor** in the workplace, the employees do calisthenics for five minutes every two hours.

The story is about a slow journey down a river flowing **languorously** to the sea.

lassitude *n.* a tired feeling, usually resulting from depression or too much work

Overcome by **lassitude**, I sat on the porch all day and watched the grass grow.

Lassitude takes hold of me whenever my dad starts telling the same boring stories about the good old days.

Myra felt overwhelming **lassitude** on the hot and humid afternoon. She couldn't even make it to the kitchen for a dish of ice cream.

lethargic *adj.* having little or no energy

It takes Herbie two hours to shake the lifeless feeling of a **lethargic** Monday morning.

Sunday mornings make Otto feel **lethargic**. He rarely stirs from his bed until after noon.

With the **lethargy** lifted, he turns into a human dynamo.

sedentary *adj.* having to do with sitting around a lot

Polly has a **sedentary** desk job. She sits all day in front of a computer screen.

A **sedentary** lifestyle caused Paul to become fat and flabby. He vows to start exercising soon.

Keith needs to keep moving. A **sedentary** day leaves him feeling like a marshmallow.

sluggish *adj.* slow and lazy

The drain in the bathtub is **sluggish**. It takes 10 minutes for the water to empty.

According to Coach Meers, a candy bar will keep you from being **sluggish** during practice.

Sluggishness must run in the family. His brother moves like a snail, too.

soporific *adj.* sleep-inducing; sleepy

A sweet, sugary dessert is as **soporific** as a sleeping pill for Dad. Ten minutes after dinner, he's out like a light.

Driving on a flat interstate highway for a long time is **soporific**. I, for one, have a hard time staying awake.

Coffee is a good anti-**soporific**. At least, it keeps me awake.

stagnant *adj.* lacking movement or energy

A **stagnant** career is one that is not going anywhere.

"Books will keep your mind from **stagnating**," said the teacher.

The still surfaces of **stagnant** pools and ponds encourage the growth of algae.

torpid *adj.* lacking energy; relating to inactivity; feeling sluggish

It was hot and muggy—a **torpid**, sleep-inducing day.

Harold felt too **torpid** to do anything but sit on the beach and count the waves.

Lying in the sun, a sweet **torpidity** overcame me, and I soon fell asleep.

MEMORY TIPS

Use these mnemonics (memory devices) to boost your vocabulary. Make up your own memory clues for words in this lesson that are personally challenging. Add these tips—and your own—to your Vocabulary Notebook. Remember, vocabulary building is key to increasing your score on the verbal SAT I.

indolence Simply link this word to *idleness* (laziness). After all, both words have three syllables and sound similar. Notice that *idle* can be spelled from the letters contained in **indolence**. Write InDoLEnce in your Vocabulary Notebook.

languor Since **languor** is a weak, tired feeling, people who feel languor tend to just hang around or *linger* a lot. Say this chant three times in a row to fix in your mind the meaning of this word: "In **languor**, I linger. In **languor**, I linger. In **languor**, I linger."

sluggish Think: Moving "like a slug!" We've all seen slugs gliding along on our patios and walkways. They are s—l—o—w-moving."

stagnant Let the *sta* at the beginning of this word make you think of *staying*, like staying in one place because there's no motion or because there's no energy to move around.

MATCHING

Match the vocabulary words in Column A with *one or more* of their defining characteristics appearing in Column B.

Column A	Column B
1. sedentary	a. slow-moving
2. soporific	b. feeling tired
3. sluggish	c. sitting around a lot
4. languid	d. sleep-inducing
5. indolent	e. lazy

SAT I-STYLE ANALOGIES

First, express a clear and concise relationship between the two given terms. Next, select the pair in the answer choices that *most closely* shares a similar relationship.

1. ENERGETIC : INDOLENT
   a. driven : jumpy
   b. new : threadbare
   c. grumpy : lost
   d. under : heaping
   e. quick : pensive

2. NOMAD : SEDENTARY
   a. messenger : lazy
   b. juror : pristine
   c. imposter : known
   d. reporter : lively
   e. operator : shaky

3. DROWSY : SOPORIFIC
   a. high : nimble
   b. grand : bleak
   c. candid : round
   d. lit : blazing
   e. cold : frigid

4. STAGNANT : DYNAMIC
   a. hinged : level
   b. numbered : listed
   c. folded : sleek
   d. dull : vibrant
   e. immobile : pelting

5. LIVELY : LETHARGIC
   a. gaunt : profuse
   b. public : private
   c. striped : spotted
   d. wild : obscure
   e. poignant : grueling

WORDS IN CONTEXT

Based on the context in which each **bold** word is used, identify the word usage of each sentence as either C (Correct) or I (Incorrect).

1. Languid people are likely to simply hang around.

2. Soporific vitamins boost athletic performance.

3. A bad attitude is necessarily a sign of sluggishness.

4. Ms. Green's bad knee makes her lifestyle increasingly sedentary.

5. Indolence is bliss for someone who dislikes work.

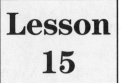
IS THERE ANYTHING I CAN DO FOR YOU, MASTER?

Words Relating to Humility and Obedience

compliant fawning obsequious servile slavish submissive subordinate subservient sycophant toady

---

compliant *adj.* yielding, submissive

Ms. Hayes prefers **compliant** students, those who'll do everything they are told.

If you **comply** with the school rules, you won't get into trouble.

Rose always **complies** with Charles's requests. She never says no.

fawning *adj.* gaining the favor of another by acting overly kind or by flattery

Mike advised me to stop **fawning** over Dawn. "She'll like you just as well even if you don't overindulge her," he said.

Fawning is a form of manipulation to win favors and get what you want from others.

As a **fawning** advisor to the Queen, Peters told Her Majesty only what she wanted to hear.

obsequious *adj.* obeying or performing a service for someone in an overly attentive manner

Uriah practiced **obsequiousness** by always telling others what a privilege it was to be of service to them.

Some teachers prefer **obsequious** students who fawn over them.

Hoping for a big tip, the waiter oozed **obsequiousness**, constantly flattering me and calling me "sir."

servile *adj.* slave-like; very humble and submissive

Roy has no right to treat you like a **servile** lackey. You are not his slave or valet.

I hate having a **servile** job. It's not in my nature to bow to the whims of others.

Susan's **servility** caused her to cater to everyone's desires but her own.

slavish *adj.* slave-like; overly humble; involving very hard work

Nicole worked **slavishly** in the kitchen preparing dinner for thirty guests.

Harry followed Sally around, **slavishly** attending to her every need.

Don had a **slavish** sidekick who did the dirty work and devoted himself to Don's well-being.

submissive *adj.* voluntarily obeying another; humble

Lauren was attracted to **submissive** friends, people who'd do everything she asked of them.

Over time, Lenny learned to be less **submissive**. He actually stood up to George once in a while.

A recruit has to be **submissive** to the sergeant or he's going to get into big trouble.

subordinate *adj.* inferior; lower in rank or status

In a sentence, a **subordinate** (dependent) clause depends on the main (independent) clause for its meaning.

The sailor was accused of **insubordination** after defying the lieutenant's order.

For the sake of good discipline, officers are forbidden to fraternize with their **subordinate** colleagues.

subservient *adj.* obedient; obsequious

In my grandmother's day, a wife was expected to be **subservient** to her husband.

Ricky asked **subserviently**, "May I please be excused, sir, for just a minute or two?"

The apprentice played a **subservient** role, trying to serve his master in every way.

sycophant *n.* a self-server who tries to gain the favor of others through the use of flattery or by being overattentive

The king couldn't distinguish the honest advisers from the **sycophants** who flattered him for personal gain.

Myron couldn't get a promotion on his merits, so he got one by being a **sycophant** to his boss.

Jason made a **sycophantic** speech full of praise and flattery for the chairman.

toady *n.* a flatterer; a sycophant

Hoping to win the coach's favor, James became the coach's **toady**.

If Mary were less of a **toady**, she wouldn't follow the teacher around so much.

Volunteering to wash the coach's car shows what a **toady** Karen has become.

MEMORY TIPS

Use these mnemonics (memory devices) to boost your vocabulary. Make up your own memory clues for words in this lesson that are personally challenging. Add these tips—and your own—to your Vocabulary Notebook.

servile, slavish These vocabulary words *contain* the keys to their definitions! Servile, servant-like. Slavish, slave-like.

submissive, subordinate, subservient The prefix *sub-*, meaning *below* or *under*, is key to these vocabulary words. Think of additional words you know, like submarine, subhuman, substitute, and subzero.

MATCHING

Match the vocabulary words in Column A with *one or more* of their defining characteristics appearing in Column B.

Column A	Column B
1. toady d	a. slave-like
2. sycophant b	b. a brownnoser
3. subservient e	c. lower in rank
4. subordinate c	d. flatterer
5. slavish a	e. obedient

SAT I-STYLE ANALOGIES

First, express a clear and concise relationship between the two given terms. Next, select the pair in the answer choices that *most closely* shares a similar relationship.

1. DISOBEDIENT : SUBMISSIVE
   a. disrespectful : insolent
   b. dismembered : slighted
   c. disputed : repeated
   d. dismissed : released
   e. dismayed : encouraged

2. FAWNING : COMPLY
   a. yawning : exhaust
   b. screeching : evade
   c. mystifying : bewilder
   d. yearning : give up
   e. flowing : force

3. SLAVE : SUBMISSIVE
   a. slaughterer : blue
   b. slanderer : grim
   c. sleigh rider : sunken
   d. sleepyhead : drowsy
   e. sleuth : tactful

4. SERVILE : TOADY
   a. virile : newscaster
   b. nimble : frog
   c. brusque : prince
   d. powerful : magnate
   e. obliged : skeleton

5. PEON : SUBSERVIENT
   a. correspondent : general
   b. diner : voracious
   c. pollster : instinctive
   d. newborn : inexperienced
   e. idler : wandering

WORDS IN CONTEXT

Based on the context in which each **bold** word is used, identify the word usage of each sentence as either C (Correct) or I (Incorrect).

1. My subservient roommate always demands her way.

2. Fawning over another makes the object of your attention feel worthless.

3. Always busy, a toady is likely to get burned out.

4. In the classroom, a sycophant might be called a "brownnoser."

5. It's surprising to witness how Harold, towering a foot and a half over his wife, acts so submissively toward his mate.

Review Exercises / Lessons 11–15

NAME THAT CLUSTER

To the left of the groups of words, put the Roman numeral that corresponds with these theme (or cluster) titles:

Words Relating to . . .

I. Lacking Energy or Movement
II. Harmful
III. Humility and Obedience
IV. Lacking Interest or Emotion
V. Criticizing, Disapproving, or Scolding

Cluster Title _____   1. virulent, deleterious, pernicious, baneful, nefarious

Cluster Title _____   2. lethargic, sedentary, lassitude, indolent, torpid

Cluster Title _____   3. censure, castigate, disparage, condemn, rebuke

Cluster Title _____   4. submissive, toady, fawning, slavish, compliant

Cluster Title _____   5. nonchalant, remote, phlegmatic, stolid, impassive

---

SENTENCE COMPLETIONS

Read the sentence through carefully. Then from the five vocabulary words given in parentheses, circle the word that fits *best*.

1. Mr. McKee spent five hours every night in his recliner, watching television. His evenings were _____.
(malicious, compliant, sedentary, stolid, aloof)

2. After eating too many sweets, Kipper felt _____. He just didn't feel like getting off the couch for *anything*.
(sluggish, remote, ominous, subordinate, fawning)

3. The youngest child, Anna, jumped at her three older brothers' commands. She played a _____ role in the family.
   (phlegmatic, baneful, odious, submissive, listless)

4. "Stop _____ all over your father!" yelled Mom. "*He* can get up and get himself a Diet Coke for once!"
   (detrimental, languid, fawning, toady, stagnating)

5. "Coating people's cars with raw egg and smashing pumpkins on front stoops is _____ even when it's Halloween," our neighbor stated firmly.
   (torpid, compliant, indifferent, obsequious, nefarious)

6. A (An) _____ youth, Tyler lounges around all day long in his typical, _____ manner.
   indolent...sycophantic
   effervescent...panegyric
   submissive...baneful
   sluggish...nefarious
   lethargic...sedentary

7. Although Patty comes across as _____ when it comes to nature and the outdoors, she is actually a (an) _____ gardener.
   deleterious...submissive
   compliant...zealous
   stolid...listless
   apathetic...avid
   castigating...odious

ONE DOESN'T BELONG

Three of the words in each grouping relate to each other somehow. Cross off the one word that does not belong with the others. For a challenge, write the word that does not belong on the line below, and try your best to define that word. *Note:* Some of the words have been taken from definitions or exercises that appear within the lessons.

1. deprecate   impugn   rebuff   iniquitous

   _____ means _____

2. stolid   subordinate   indifferent   detached

   _____ means _____

3. toady   sycophant   impassive   fawning

   _____ means _____

4. loathsome   odious   nefarious   obsequious

   _____ means _____

5. aloof   berate   disinterested   listless

   _____ means _____

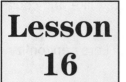

Lesson 16

HOW WONDERFUL! HOW EXCITING!

Words Relating to Enthusiasm and Passion

---

ardent avid ebullient effervescent exuberant fanatical fervent impassioned vibrant zealous

---

ardent *adj.* full of passion and emotion

Ardent soccer fans never miss a game.

John and Sherrie's embrace was more than a casual hug; it was an **ardent** show of affection.

For their extraordinary service, the volunteers deserve **ardent** thanks.

avid *adj.* showing enthusiasm; ardent

Walt is an **avid** hiker; he never misses a chance to hit the trail.

An **avid** skier, Sue will drive for hours to be where the snow is.

For years my dad has been an **avid** golfer, out on the links every weekend.

ebullient *adj.* filled with a bubbly excitement, as if boiling over with excitement

The audience became just as enthusiastic about following the diet as the **ebullient** speaker was in describing it.

His **ebullience** was infectious. Everyone left the room filled with excitement about the rafting trip.

Having made a hole in one, Tiger could hardly contain his **ebullience**.

effervescent *adj.* lively; full of uplifted spirit; vivacious

Distressed over losing the car keys, Beth was less **effervescent** than usual.

The root beer had lost its **effervescence** and tasted like bad cough syrup.

Laura is quiet and subdued, but her twin Lara epitomizes **effervescence**.

exuberant *adj.* overflowing with vitality and good spirits

As a night owl, Amelia feels most **exuberant** between ten o'clock and midnight.

Worry and anxiety can put a damper on even the most **exuberant** personality.

The next morning he leaped from bed **exuberantly**, anticipating the adventures of the day.

fanatical *adj.* full of great enthusiasm or devotion

Clark is a **fanatical** bowler. His head is filled with thoughts of strikes and spares, balls and alleys.

Louise's mom is **fanatical** about cleaning the house. She won't let you in the house unless you take your shoes off.

I don't eat red meat, but I'm not **fanatical** about it.

fervent *adj.* filled with passion or intensity

The minister asked her congregation to pray **fervently** for the safe return of the lost child.

He's a **fervent** cat breeder. Nothing is as important to him as raising cats.

She's a nut for crossword puzzles, but she hasn't always been so **fervent** about doing them.

impassioned *adj.* filled with passionate emotion

The defense attorney made an **impassioned** speech to the jury, but the jury remained unmoved by his emotional words.

Because Tino's **impassioned** words struck Maria's heart, she agreed to marry him.

King Henry's **impassioned** speech to his troops raised their morale and contributed to their victory in battle.

vibrant *adj.* lively; full of vitality

Marilyn and Curt are an unlikely couple. She's so **vibrant**, and he's as quiet as a corpse.

Although the bright hues clash sometimes, all of Diana's clothes have **vibrant** colors.

His **vibrant** teaching keeps the class lively.

zealous *adj.* filled with enthusiasm; fervent

A **zealous** bodybuilder, Derek works out in the weight room during every spare moment.

If everyone were as **zealous** a worker as Scott, there would be no need for a supervisor.

Jorge is a **zealous** reader of mysteries. As soon as he finishes one book, he starts reading the next.

MEMORY TIPS

Use these mnemonics (memory devices) to boost your vocabulary. Make up your own memory clues for words in this lesson that are personally challenging. Add these tips—and your own—to your Vocabulary Notebook. Remember, vocabulary building is key to increasing your score on the verbal SAT I.

ebullient Let *bull* remind you of strong. Next, let the initial *e* stand for enthusiasm or excitement. "Strong enthusiasm/excitement" is a concise working definition for this vocabulary word.

fanatical Is this a new vocabulary word for you? I bet it's not. You already know what a *fan* is, right? Think of sports fan, Britney Spears fan, NSync fan, and so on. Simply link your understanding of *fan* to the meaning of **fanatical** (acting like a *fan*.)

fervent Scramble the first five letters to get *fever*. Next, connect *fever* (something hot, burning) to "full of passion," which is the kernel definition of **fervent**. Write **fervent** in red ink in your Vocabulary Notebook. Use red for passion.

MATCHING

Match the vocabulary words in Column A with *one or more* of their defining characteristics appearing in Column B.

Column A	Column B
1. ebullient	a. filled with passion
2. ardent	b. overly devoted
3. impassioned	c. bubbling with enthusiasm
4. effervescent	d. avid
5. fanatical	e. full of lively spirit

SAT I-STYLE ANALOGIES

First, express a clear and concise relationship between the two given terms. Next, select the pair in the answer choices that *most closely* shares a similar relationship.

1. AVID : DEVOTEE
   a. slender : pushover
   b. ignoble : leader
   c. nocturnal : owl
   d. yearning : elder
   e. fearful : moose

2. ARDENT : FERVENT
   a. hands-on : tactful
   b. united : divided
   c. oscillating : wavering
   d. fussy : light
   e. grounded : shaded

3. VIGOR : VERVE
   a. heroism : didacticism
   b. brusqueness : briskness
   c. flippancy : falsity
   d. grace : liberty
   e. will : inertia

4. DYNAMO : EXUBERANT
   a. authority : languid
   b. counselor : quixotic
   c. junior : guileless
   d. subordinate : inferior
   e. domestic : obliging

5. IMPASSIONED : INDIFFERENT
   a. neutral : cursory
   b. idle : inactive
   c. upstanding : youthful
   d. bipolar : central
   e. unfaltering : undecided

WORDS IN CONTEXT

Based on the context in which each **bold** word is used, identify the word usage of each sentence as either C (Correct) or I (Incorrect).

1. Ana's impassioned letter lacks strong emotion.

2. The fervent sports manager neglected his leadership responsibilities.

3. Envy is a likely character flaw of a zealous individual.

4. A fervent NSync follower, Gus never missed one of their concerts or MTV specials.

5. John, an ardent fast food entrepreneur, steadfastly pursued his aims and goals despite many setbacks.

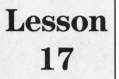

Lesson 17

LIKE A MULE

Words Relating to Being Stubborn

adamant dogmatic hidebound intractable obdurate obstinate recalcitrant resolve unwavering unyielding willful

adamant *adj.* unwilling to bend; unyielding

Although the invitation said dress was formal, Chucky was **adamant** about wearing track shoes to the prom.

Dad's **adamant** tone convinced him there was no chance he could go dressed like that.

Mom **adamantly** refused my request for Coca-Cola at breakfast.

dogmatic *adj.* strongly opinionated; rigid; dictatorial

Dogmatic Doug was so set in his convictions that he would not even listen to viewpoints that were expressed by another person.

Dogmatic religious beliefs are rooted in firm principles and rigid codes of conduct.

Pleading for permission to sleep at her friend's house, Beth sulked when her mother answered with a **dogmatic** "No!" This topic was not open for discussion.

hidebound *adj.* strongly-opinionated; narrow-mindedly stubborn

Dad is a **hidebound** Boston fan; he has rooted for the Red Sox all his life.

A **hidebound** vegetarian, Vera turned down a free hot dog at the ball game.

Hidebound and set in his ways, Grandpa will not eat anything for dinner unless it's meat and potatoes.

intractable *adj.* stubborn; hard to manage

Because neither his teachers nor his counselor could control Ivan's **intractable** behavior, he was sent to the psychologist for testing.

An **intractable** nature cannot easily be tamed.

Rose forced open the **intractable** window with a screwdriver.

obdurate *adj.* resistant to persuasion or softening; stubbornly persistent in wrongdoing

The killer showed no remorse for his deed. For being **obdurate**, he was sentenced to life in prison.

Steve stuck to his opinion **obdurately** in spite of evidence that proved him wrong.

Senator McCain was unwilling to compromise. By being **obdurate**, he finally got the bill passed.

obstinate *adj.* stubborn; inflexible

Despite an allergy to chocolate, Charlotte **obstinately** refused to give up her daily bag of M&M's.

"Don't be so **obstinate**," pleaded Mother. "Try having an open mind instead."

The teacher **obstinately** refused to believe that Harold wrote the paper himself.

recalcitrant *adj.* stubborn, disobedient; defiant

The **recalcitrant** boy in the back row refused to turn off his cell phone during class.

In spite of the law, many **recalcitrant** drivers resist putting on seat belts.

The usher asked the moviegoers to form an orderly line, but the **recalcitrant** crowd wouldn't budge.

resolve *n.* firmness, determination

"Don't doubt my **resolve**," said Holly. "I definitely will become a famous fashion designer one day."

"Rely on your inner **resolve** to just say no to drugs," said nurse Betty.

After a disastrous first marking period, Shawn **resolved** to do better during the next one.

unwavering *adj.* firm and determined

Trudy's **unwavering** desire to lose weight kept her on the all-pineapple diet for a month.

Hoping for an 800 on the verbal section of the SAT I, Dave **unwaveringly** studied every vocabulary word in the book.

Instead of abandoning the president in time of trouble, many people stood by him **unwaveringly**.

unyielding *adj.* stubborn; inflexible

Whenever Cecile asked her father to buy her a car, her dad gave her the same **unyielding** answer: "Not a chance!"

Ms. Grace practices **unyielding** courtesy. She never fails to thank a student for handing in a homework assignment.

The troops fought with an **unyielding** ferocity, never stopping until they had won the battle.

willful *adj.* stubborn

It makes no sense to **willfully** ignore the evidence against smoking.

Jill knows that she's a **willful** brat who insists on always getting her way.

Vandalizing the poster was no accident. It was done **willfully**.

MEMORY TIPS

Use these mnemonics (memory devices) to boost your vocabulary. Make up your own memory clues for words in this lesson that are personally challenging. Add these tips—and your own—to your Vocabulary Notebook.

dogmatic The stem for this word is *dogma*. A dogma is a rigid set of beliefs or principles, or a set of beliefs held as unquestionable truth. Therefore, a person who is **dogmatic** has his or her beliefs and ideas rooted in dogma.

hidebound Did you know that "hide" is another word for leather (buckskin, pigskin, etc.)? Imagine a person wrapped tight in "hide," so set in her opinion that she won't budge. Picture it? In other words, a **hidebound** individual is unwavering, unyielding, unwilling to "give a little." Someone **hidebound** is stubborn, set in his or her ways.

obdurate, obstinate Learn these two words meaning *stubborn* as a pair. After all, they both start off with *ob*, and they both have three syllables. In addition, if you study or speak Italian, you may know that "dura" means hard. So **obdurate** means *hard-headed*, which is slang for *stubborn*. Whether you know some Italian or not, it's smart to always consider the vocabulary you know from your second or third language. Memory clues that are formed from foreign language connections are very effective and fun.

SAT I-STYLE ANALOGIES

First, express a clear and concise relationship between the two given terms. Next, select the pair in the answer choices that *most closely* shares a similar relationship.

1. OBDURATE : YIELDING
   a. trim : slim
   b. ambiguous : uncanny
   c. hesitant : rash
   d. miserable : detached
   e. lost : ponderous

2. DOCILE : INTRACTABLE
   a. impudent : light-hearted
   b. restrained : swerving
   c. grand : substantiative
   d. thoughtful : penetrating
   e. crude : polite

3. MULE : OBSTINATE
   a. cat : humane
   b. fox : sly
   c. bird : flighty
   d. eagle : blissful
   e. cow : dairy

4. WAVERING : UNCERTAIN
   a. germane : relevant
   b. clueless : tired
   c. carping : cheating
   d. experienced : mindful
   e. monitored : mastered

5. HEADSTRONG : ADAMANT
   a. related : hindered
   b. brainy : bleak
   c. desperate : vindicated
   d. blunt : aware
   e. kind : compassionate

WORDS IN CONTEXT

Based on the context in which each **bold** word is used, identify the word usage of each sentence as either C (Correct) or I (Incorrect).

1. Once Brandon has his mind set, there's no changing it; he's an unwavering young man.

2. Intractable individuals are the easiest to control.

3. When it comes to homework, Mother is adamant about it getting done sometime after school or, perhaps, soon after dinner. Otherwise, Mom wants it finished by 11 P.M.

4. An obstinate child is easily led by his peers.

5. Resolved to get her first children's book published, Lillian set aside a minimum of five hours a day for writing and marketing.

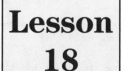

Lesson 18

SOUND SENSATIONS
Words Relating to Sound

---

acoustics cacophony clamor din discordant euphony
mellifluous raucous strident vociferous

---

acoustics *n.* the quality of sound, pertaining to how it is heard based on the quality and structure of the room

At first the sound inside Philharmonic Hall was flat, but after the renovation, the **acoustics** were perfect.

The sound track of the film was extraordinary. Whoever handled the sound must have been an **acoustic** genius.

Always fascinated by sound, Ernest studied to be an **acoustical** engineer.

cacophony *n.* lack of harmony; loud and unpleasant noise; a racket

The clash of metal on the rocks created a **cacophony** that was hard to bear.

The mix of harsh sounds in the streets of the city creates a **cacophony**.

Unlike old-fashioned melodic music, ultra-modern music often consists of lots of **cacophonous** sounds.

clamor *n.* unpleasant sound; noise

The **clamor** of a crowing rooster and clucking hens woke up the farmer.

How can I concentrate with that **clamor** of pots and dishes going on in the kitchen?

Earphones muffled the **clamor**, allowing Davy to listen to the music in peace.

din *n.* ongoing loud sound; noise

When Bernie hit the grand slam, the **din** in Yankee Stadium could be heard all the way to City Hall.

The farmyard **din** astonished Farmer Jones. He had never heard all his animals bellowing so loudly.

The **din** of the bulldozer at work next door made it impossible for us to hear each other.

discordant *adj.* lacking harmony or agreement

Instead of beautiful melodies, Berg wrote **discordant** notes that grate on the ear.

All agreed to the decision until Paul brought up the **discordant** fact that our group lacked the authority to make such decisions.

The first sign of **discord** between Jenny and Harvey was the shouting match they had one day after school.

euphony *n.* pleasing sound

While I rested in bed under a cozy blanket, the **euphony** of raindrops on the roof soon lulled me to sleep.

Junior's violin screeching sounded **euphonious** only to his parents. Everyone else covered their ears.

The sound of a school bell, while irritating to others, is **euphony** to me.

mellifluous *adj.* sweet and smooth sounding

Mother's **mellifluous** singing voice was so sweet and soothing that the baby fell asleep in seconds.

Because of his **mellifluous** voice, Grant was hired as a radio announcer.

The **mellifluous** tones of an Irish tenor floated through my hotel window in Dublin.

raucous *adj.* coarse-sounding; loud and unruly

The **raucous** band prevented us from hearing each other speak, so we used gestures and pantomime.

As the princess's motorcade came closer, the crowd grew **raucous**, and when she arrived, the din was impossible.

The **raucous** strikers yelled obscenities at passersby.

strident *adj.* shrill; high-pitched

> Joe started off with some harsh words that set a **strident** tone for the whole meeting.

> It's hard to take the sound of the **strident** school bell so early in the morning.

> The geese flew south, leaving the sound of their **strident** honks behind them.

vociferous *adj.* loud and noisy regarding one's own voice, especially shouting; demandingly clamorous

> Danny **vociferously** denied cutting class. He wouldn't stop shouting about it for hours.

> The **vociferous** crowd noisily demanded that the store open its doors. "Open up or else," they shouted.

> I couldn't help overhearing the **vociferous** altercation that took place in the waiting room. It was too loud to ignore.

MEMORY TIPS

Use these mnemonics (memory devices) to boost your vocabulary. Make up your own memory clues for words in this lesson that are personally challenging. Add these tips—and your own—to your Vocabulary Notebook.

cacophony, euphony These words both contain *phon*, which is the root having to do with sound. Knowledge of this root alone is very helpful in recognizing the meanings of these words. Prefixes are helpful to know, too. *Eu-* indicates *good*, as in euphoria and euphemism, for example. (Look these up!) *Caco-*, a derivative of the Greek "kakos," indicates *bad*. Did you know that cacography means bad handwriting and/or poor spelling?

mellifluous Repeat this chant aloud three times in a row: "**Mellifluous** melodies, **mellifluous** melodies, **mellifluous** melodies." This alliterative chant should remind you that melodies are sweet-sounding, smooth-sounding; in other words, **mellifluous**. Write this chant three times in your Vocabulary Notebook.

MATCHING

Match the vocabulary words in Column A with *one or more* of their defining characteristics appearing in Column B.

Column A

1. euphony
2. din
3. cacophonous
4. acoustics
5. vociferous
6. mellifluous

Column B

a. relating to the science of sound
b. harsh-sounding
c. having to do with loud voices
d. consistent, loud noise
e. pleasing sound
f. smooth-sounding

SAT I-STYLE ANALOGIES

First, express a clear and concise relationship between the two given terms. Next, select the pair in the answer choices that *most closely* shares a similar relationship.

1. DIN : NOISE

  a. jargon : junket
  b. bolster : pillow
  c. treaty : novel
  d. tableau : trinket
  e. hangar : lentil

2. VOCIFEROUS : RIOTERS

  a. vindictive : avengers
  b. bereaved : stragglers
  c. learned : idols
  d. weary : hikers
  e. concerned : peons

3. SQUEAL : STRIDENT

  a. growl : grim
  b. yelp : nasty
  c. pop : blunt
  d. cough : warm
  e. uproar : loud

4. CACOPHONY : EUPHONY

  a. volt : mitt
  b. bear : boor
  c. polygamy : monogamy
  d. nomination : election
  e. cultivation : cubbyhole

5. ACOUSTICS : SOUND QUALITY

  a. gymnastics : body movements
  b. forensics : foreign lands
  c. euphemisms: elder traits
  d. relics : real inventions
  e. hieroglyphics : sea formations

WORDS IN CONTEXT

Based on the context in which each **bold** word is used, identify the word usage of each sentence as either C (Correct) or I (Incorrect).

1. The **acoustics** enjoyed at Avery Fisher Hall are among the best world-wide.

2. Upon entering her friend's home, the woman let out a **strident** "Yooo-Whoooo!" that startled the homeowner.

3. Do you prefer peaceful evenings or **clamorous** mornings?

4. Do you like to **din** more so at friends' houses or at restaurants?

5. The **euphony** of the heavenly violins lingered pleasantly in Mia's memory for hours after the concert's conclusion.

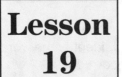

acclaim accolade adulate esteem eulogize exalt extol laud
panegyrize revere venerate

acclaim *v.* to express strong approval or praise; hail

He's an accomplished artist, **acclaimed** by all the critics.

Dad was happy to hear his son's talent **acclaimed** by his teachers.

It is a hit play, but in spite of all the **acclaim** it has received, I didn't think much of it.

accolade *n.* an award given as a sign of appreciation or respect

The Broadway diva received many **accolades** for her stellar performance.

Inclusion in the Zagat's restaurant guide is one of the greatest **accolades** any fine eatery can receive.

For the young soccer player, each trophy that his team received was an **accolade**, commending both their team spirit and dedication.

adulate *v.* to praise or flatter too greatly; fawn over

Students who are **adulated** often end up with swelled heads, but not Sean. In spite of the awe he inspires, he's very modest.

Personally, I don't **adulate** him, but I admire and respect his many talents.

Sean received the **adulation** for being both the valedictorian and the school's outstanding athlete.

esteem *v.* to value highly; to have great regard for

Bernard is a well-known philanthropist. Far and wide he is highly **esteemed** for his generosity.

Ms. Boyd was **esteemed** by both her employers and her colleagues for all her hard work over the years.

To show how highly they **esteemed** her, they gave her $1 million in stock options when she retired.

eulogize *v.* to praise, as in a eulogy; to say good things about

Loretta knew Mike well and **eulogized** the good deeds for which he'll be remembered.

The minister's sermon comforted the grieving family, who appreciated hearing him **eulogize** Grandma's kind and loving spirit.

The introduction sounds like a **eulogy**. While full of praise for the author, it is written in the past tense as though he had already died.

exalt *v.* to praise or glorify; to lift up in status, dignity, power

As the honored leader of the organization, she was **exalted** by the members.

Once **exalted** by the Russian people, Stalin is now a devil in their eyes.

The church plans to **exalt** Mother Teresa by making her a saint.

extol *v.* to praise highly; laud

Extolling the efforts of students never fails to motivate them to keep up the good work.

Those who **extolled** JFK in the past ate their words when some of his less than admirable qualities became public.

The piano teacher **extolled** Johnny's playing, but Johnny's performance revealed that he didn't deserve such high praise.

laud *v.* to praise; extol

He **lauded** my efforts to help, but I didn't think the praise was sincere.

The **lauditory** comments on the back cover suggest that this is a terrific book.

To fly solo across the Atlantic in 1927 was a remarkable achievement for which Lindbergh was **lauded** by the people everywhere.

panegyrize *v.* to praise a person or event in a formal speech or in writing; to praise highly

> Mr. Don was asked to say a word in praise of the artist, but he got carried away and **panegyrized** the embarrassed young woman.

> As best man at the wedding, Luke **panegyrized** the happy couple.

> Before presenting the award, Miss America **panegyrized** this year's winner.

revere *v.* to regard highly with love and respect

> Ivan's essays were **revered** for their far-reaching wisdom and clarity of thought.

> To **revere** the Founding Fathers is part of the formula for making a speech on the Fourth of July.

> The Joads **revered** the land, but the landlord didn't care how much they loved it, and chose to evict them.

venerate *v.* to feel or show deep respect for, especially due to age or tradition; to honor

> Most religions expect believers to **venerate** old customs and traditions.

> The scholar, now old and frail, was still **venerated** by his former colleagues.

> Few people still **venerate** lawyers and politicians merely because of the positions they hold.

MEMORY TIPS

Use these mnemonics (memory devices) to boost your vocabulary. Make up your own memory clues for words in this lesson that are challenging for you. Add these tips—and your own—to your Vocabulary Notebook.

laud If you know *applaud*, then simply connect the new word **laud** to the word you already know, *app<u>laud</u>*. The meanings of these two verbs are closely connected.

revere You remember Paul Revere from American History, right? Now, I'm sure you'll agree that it's only right to respect, or **revere**, one of our nation's Founding Fathers!

Another tip: You can repeat this chant to yourself over and over "**Revere** the Reverend. **Revere** the Reverend. **Revere** the Reverend."

MATCHING

Match the vocabulary words in Column A with *one or more* of their defining characteristics appearing in Column B.

Column A	Column B
1. acclaim	a. to praise in formal writing
2. adulate	b. to praise highly
3. revere	c. to glorify or lift up in dignity
4. eulogize	d. to regard highly with respect
5. exalt	e. to overly praise; fawn over
6. panegyrize	f. to speak words in praise of someone at a funeral or mass

SAT I-STYLE ANALOGIES

First, express a clear and concise relationship between the two given terms. Next, select the pair in the answer choices that *most closely* shares a similar relationship.

1. REVERE : PRAISE
   a. love : dispute
   b. abhor : detest
   c. appreciate : ensue
   d. loathe : dislike
   e. feel : desire

2. SYCHOPHANT : ADULATE
   a. tyro : excel
   b. skeptic : believe
   c. miser : share
   d. zealot : rearrange
   e. altruist : donate

3. EULOGY : WORDS
   a. melody : notes
   b. sunset : clouds
   c. vapor : increments
   d. essay : narrators
   e. speech : interruptions

4. SELF-EFFACEMENT : SELF-ESTEEM
   a. arrogance : conundrum
   b. ego : enigma
   c. humility : pride
   d. affliction : affection
   e. inversion : utopia

5. EXTOL : LAUD
   a. react : rescind
   b. assert : state
   c. nullify : exclude
   d. amass : scatter
   e. disperse : disappear

WORDS IN CONTEXT

Based on the context in which each **bold** word is used, identify the word usage of each sentence as either C (Correct) or I (Incorrect).

1. Generally speaking, people who esteem themselves are emotionally healthy.

2. When Kevin's essay was acclaimed as exemplary, he was thrilled.

3. It is recommended to laud false acts of kindness.

4. One way to venerate grandparents is to listen to their stories of "the good old days."

5. Praised by all for her genuine and golden heart, Terri was exalted to the realm of earth angels.

Lesson 20

ENOUGH IS ENOUGH
Words Relating to More Than Enough

> ample copious lavish myriad plethora profuse prolific
> superfluous surfeit

ample *adj.* abundant; plentiful; enough or more than enough

It will be expensive to send me to college, but my parents have **ample** funds, thank goodness.

For turning in the lost wallet, Heather was given an **ample** reward of $200.

Juice and a piece of toast is an **ample** breakfast for me, although Mom thinks I ought to eat more.

copious *adj.* abundant; much; plentiful

I couldn't attend the meeting, so Julie took **copious** notes. Now I know everything that happened there.

The director explained the camp's procedures in **copious** detail, far more than I needed or wanted to know.

It rained **copiously** day and night, leaving the streets flooded.

lavish (from Lesson 8) *adj.* abundant; in excess

My **lavish** weekend excursion resulted in a huge bill on my dad's Visa card.

Trudy's reaction to the meager furnishings in the dorm room suggests that she's used to more **lavish** living quarters.

On the cruise we ate **lavishly**, enjoying huge meals three times a day and snacks in between.

myriad *adj.* or *n.* countless; a very large number

Kenny failed the test by making **myriad** mistakes in addition and subtraction.

New York has a **myriad** of restaurants. The number and variety is astounding.

Myriad airplanes filled the sky. It's a wonder they didn't crash into one another.

plethora *n.* excess; abundance

The kindergarten room is crowded with a **plethora** of materials and equipment.

There used to be a **plethora** of teachers, but now there is a shortage.

Considering the **plethora** of ways to get lost en route, it's a marvel that you got here so soon.

profuse *adj.* abundant; more than enough

Please accept my **profuse** thanks for your hospitality. Your graciousness knows no bounds.

Herman bled so **profusely** from the wound that he almost lost consciousness.

The **profusion** of options in our curriculum gives students many choices to make.

prolific *adj.* abundant; producing a great deal; fertile

Despite Marvin's **prolific** fiction writing, he never shared any of his many short stories with others.

A **prolific** artist, Caroline painted hundreds of watercolors and landscapes in her lifetime.

Drew's patience and care in tending to his garden led to a **prolific** harvest of basil, tomatoes, and zucchini.

superfluous *adj.* overabundant; more than is needed; unnecessary

Since the birthday card was sufficient recognition of the big day, the gift was **superfluous**.

I understood the rules before the race started, so the coach's instructions were **superfluous**.

Most of what I brought along for the camping trip was **superfluous**. I didn't need the majority of it.

surfeit *n.* an oversupply

A **surfeit** of donations made the drive to collect more money superfluous.

During Halloween, kids collect a **surfeit** of candy and other sweets.

A **surfeit** of wheat enables the United States to export wheat to needy countries.

MEMORY TIPS

Use these mnemonics (memory devices) to boost your vocabulary. Make up your own memory clues for words in this lesson that are personally challenging. Add these tips—and your own—to your Vocabulary Notebook. One thing you can never get enough of when preparing for the SAT I is vocabulary.

copious Let yourself see the word *copies* within **copious**, and think "lots of copies." Certainly "lots of copies" leads to the defining ideas of *abundant* and *plentiful*.

plethora Let the *ple* lead you to *plenty*. When you write **plethora** in your Vocabulary Notebook, underscore *ple* with a colored pen or marker.

superfluous The prefix *super-* means over and above. This knowledge is helpful because superfluous means "above what is needed; extra."

surfeit Like *super-*, *sur-* is also a prefix meaning over and above. So a **surfeit** is an amount over and above what is needed. Using apperception (see Introduction), link a word you most likely already know, sur-plus, to the new word, **surfeit**. These two-syllable synonyms even have the same number of letters! Solidify the meaning of **surfeit** in your memory.

MATCHING

Match the vocabulary words in Column A with *one or more* of their defining characteristics appearing in Column B.

Column A

1. surfeit
2. myriad
3. superfluous
4. ample
5. profuse

Column B

a. unnecessary
b. big number
c. glut
d. abundant
e. countless

SAT I-STYLE ANALOGIES

First, express a clear and concise relationship between the two given terms. Next, select the pair in the answer choices that *most closely* shares a similar relationship.

1. MYRIAD : FEW
   a. fraction : whole
   b. decimal : wholistic
   c. digit : singular
   d. integer : divided
   e. unit : infinite

2. PLENTIFUL : PROFUSE
   a. little : nimble
   b. high : dingy
   c. scanty : nonexistent
   d. fruitful : productive
   e. adroit : deaf

3. LIMITED : LAVISH
   a. serious : grave
   b. resonant : stiff
   c. acrid : biting
   d. yielding : lonely
   e. reclusive : extroverted

4. DEFICIT : SURFEIT
   a. glut : jaunt
   b. bonus : break
   c. era : wrongdoing
   d. plane : hovercraft
   e. decline : incline

5. GREAT AMOUNT : AMPLE
   a. small area : productive
   b. narrow space : canine
   c. uphill climb : arduous
   d. slim slope : expert
   e. little bit : easy

WORDS IN CONTEXT

Based on the context in which each **bold** word is used, identify the word usage of each sentence as either C (Correct) or I (Incorrect).

1. Joanne enjoyed ample fineries while camping in the woods.

2. Sasga feels great gratitude for her life, which brims with profuse blessings.

3. There are a plethora of reasons why I don't wish to go to Europe with you. I can name at least a dozen reasons right off the bat.

4. Myriad sleigh riders swept down the snowy hills of Terrace Village; in fact, only two sleighers were spotted.

5. Kurt spoiled his girlfriend with lavish gifts of jewelry, handbags, and perfumes.

Review Exercises / Lessons 16–20

NAME THAT CLUSTER

To the left of the groups of words, put the Roman numeral that corresponds with these theme (or cluster) titles:

Words Relating to . . .

I. Being Stubborn
II. Enthusiasm and Passion
III. More Than Enough
IV. Sound
V. Praise and Respect

Cluster Title _____ 1. mellifluous, acoustics, euphony, vociferous, discordant
Cluster Title _____ 2. avid, zealous, effervescent, ardent, fervent
Cluster Title _____ 3. laud, revere, venerate, extol, eulogize
Cluster Title _____ 4. obdurate, hidebound, obstinate, adamant, unwavering
Cluster Title _____ 5. lavish, myriad, copious, plethora, profuse

SENTENCE COMPLETIONS

Read the sentence through carefully. Then from the five vocabulary words given in parentheses, circle the word that fits *best*.

1. The grandchildren _____ Grandfather Albert not only for his infinite wisdom, but also for his family loyalty.
   (lavished, hidebound, venerated, effervesced, impassioned)

2. Jumping up and down joyfully, Miranda became increasingly _____ as she won one terrific raffle prize after another!
   (ebullient, fanatical, superficial, copious, strident)

3. Donna's _____ voice has a calming effect on the people she talks to.
(plethora, vibrant, exuberant, mellifluous, surfeit)

4. At the charity dinner, the _____ of the loudspeaker made it nearly impossible to have a conversation with the person sitting next to you.
(recalcitrant, fervent, dogged, din, adulation)

5. A(An) _____ coin collector, Connie has coins from nearly every country around the world.
(clamorous, acoustical, cacophonous, avid, esteemed)

6. To Susan's sensitive ear, the harpsichord sounds harsh and _____, whereas the piano sounds wonderfully _____.
copious...fervent
discordant...mellifluous
unyielding...obstinate
acoustical...vociferous
effervescent...ebullient

7. You can try to persuade me with _____ gifts, but I remain _____; I simply will *never* be able to see your point of view on this issue.
myriad...vibrant
venerated...clamorous
lavish...obstinate
euphonious...strident
superfluous...exuberant

ONE DOESN'T BELONG

Three of the words in each grouping relate to each other somehow. Cross off the one word that does not belong with the others. For a challenge, write the word that does not belong on the line below, and try your best to define that word. *Note:* Some of the words have been taken from definitions or exercises that appear within the lessons.

1. vivacious   vibrant   vitality   vociferous

   _____ means _____

2. dogged   effervescent   resolved   inflexible

   _____ means _____

3. copious   defiant   profuse   plethoric

   _____ means _____

4. recalcitrant   cacophonous   strident   din

   _____ means _____

5. extol   surfeit   panegyrize   esteem

   _____ means _____

MMMmmm . . . DELICIOUS!
Words Relating to Food and Hunger

> **abstemious alimentary culinary delectable emaciated epicurean glutton palatable ravenous savory voracious**

---

abstemious *adj.* holding back from eating or drinking too much

Grandpa eats like a bird. Mother fears that his **abstemious** nature may not be good for him.

With a buffet dinner that includes an Italian hero and pepperoni pizza, it is hard to be **abstemious**.

I need the willpower to be more **abstemious** if I'm going to lose 10 pounds by June.

alimentary *adj.* relating to food and nourishment

Fast foods provide little nourishment, but fresh fruits and vegetables are good for your **alimentary** health.

In biology we learned about the **alimentary** canal, the system in the body for swallowing and digesting food.

I saw an interesting program about nutrition, digestion, and other **alimentary** matters.

culinary *adj.* having to do with cooking, preparing meals

Our chef went to the **Culinary** Institute to learn all about food preparation.

Airline food is anything but a **culinary** delight.

Martha was distressed about how awful the dinner was. She called it "a **culinary** disaster."

delectable *adj.* delicious

> The aroma of fresh baked bread and other **delectable**, mouth-watering foods wafted through the house.

> For Gary, there's no more **delectable** meal than baked macaroni and cheese.

> When asked, "How's the roast beef?" Meg replied, "**Delectable**," as gravy ran down her chin.

emaciated *adj.* very, very thin due to lack of adequate food

> Winter out on the range with very little food left the cattle **emaciated**.

> Anorexia left Laura looking **emaciated**, like a victim of malnutrition.

> It is hard to look at photos of **emaciated** children who are victims of the Ruanda famine.

epicurean *adj.* having to do with relishing the pleasure of eating and drinking (*n.* epicure)

> At the reception, the table was piled high with the most delicious **epicurean** delights.

> A McDonald's cheeseburger and fries may taste good to some people, but it is not my idea of an **epicurean** meal.

> As a dyed-in-the-wool **epicure**, Clyde eats at only the very best restaurants.

glutton *n.* one who overindulges in food and drink

> Eddie proved he was a **glutton** by eating a whole pumpkin pie and a half-gallon of ice cream at one sitting.

> Rachel was such a **glutton**, she ate huge meals even when she wasn't hungry.

> I don't eat much candy, but I become a **glutton** in front of a plate of chocolate chip cookies.

palatable *adj.* pleasing to the taste buds

> This stew tastes awful. To make it more **palatable**, add salt and garlic.

Zina found Ethan's rabbit stew **unpalatable** and refused to eat it.

What do you find more **palatable**, shrimp or lobster?

ravenous *adj.* very hungry

A day spent outdoors makes me **ravenous** enough to eat a hippopotamus.

Matt is a **ravenous** eater. When he's not poking around in the refrigerator, he's exploring the pantry for snacks.

Caviar is supposedly a gourmet food, but I'd have to be **ravenous** before swallowing fish eggs.

savory *adj.* tasty or good smelling

Spices can turn a bland, tasteless dish into a **savory** one.

Don't gulp the wine as though it's a glass of soda. To **savor** it, sip slowly.

The label on the can says the soup is **savory**, but to me it has no flavor whatsoever.

voracious *adj.* greedy; gluttonous; ravenous; insatiable

Because Molly skipped breakfast and lunch, she had a **voracious** appetite at dinner.

Tucker is a **voracious** eater. Every day he polishes off a half-dozen hamburgers, a pound of potato salad, and a giant bowl of chocolate mousse.

Sally reads mysteries **voraciously**. No sooner does she finish one than she starts reading another.

MEMORY TIPS

Use these mnemonics (memory devices) to boost your vocabulary. Make up your own memory clues for words in this lesson that are personally challenging. Add these two tips—and your own—to your Vocabulary Notebook. Remember, vocabulary building is key to increasing your score on the verbal SAT I.

alimentary Recall your class work in biology and life science. Have you heard of the "alimentary canal"? If so, link your knowledge to the meaning of **alimentary**, pertaining to food and nourishment. According to Britannica online, the **alimentary canal** is the "pathway along which food travels when it is eaten and from which solid wastes are expelled." The **alimentary** canal includes the mouth, pharynx, esophagus, stomach, small and large intestines, and the anal canal.

delectable Let the sound and look of this word help you remember its meaning. After all, there's quite a resemblance between **delectable** and two of its synonyms, *delicious* and *delightful.* All three terms begin with *del* and they are similar—if not the same—in length. Write delectable, delicious, and delightful as a mini-cluster in your Vocabulary Notebook.

glutton Did you know that *glut* means "an oversupply or surplus"? If so, then your preexisting knowledge will help you remember the meaning of **glutton**, a person who indulges in a *glut*, or oversupply, of food and drink.

MATCHING

Match the vocabulary words in Column A with *one or more* of their defining characteristics appearing in Column B.

Column A	**Column B**
1. emaciated	a. greedily hungry
2. alimentary	b. an overeater
3. savory	c. extremely skinny
4. ravenous	d. having to do with cooking
5. culinary	e. having to do with nutritional needs
6. glutton	f. tasty

SAT I-STYLE ANALOGIES

First, express a clear and concise relationship between the two given terms. Next, select the pair in the answer choices that *most closely* shares a similar relationship.

1. RAVENOUS : VORACIOUS

    a. ludicrous : crazy
    b. basic : upturned
    c. prepared : defined
    d. complete : limp
    e. tactical : resolved

2. FOOD : GLUTTON

    a. delicacies : queen
    b. magic : craftsman
    c. travel : voyager
    d. money : alternate
    e. flexibility : gymnast

3. INEDIBLE : PALATABLE

    a. pleasing : pleasurable
    b. reliable : unpredictable
    c. pure : heavy
    d. blind : disciplined
    e. planned : extensive

4. NOURISHMENT : ALIMENTARY

    a. peace : stationary
    b. love : astrological
    c. news : climatic
    d. attention : studious
    e. purity : pristine

5. ABSTEMIOUS : GLUTTONOUS

    a. rigid : slim
    b. round : oval
    c. mired : drawn
    d. regal : royal
    e. light : ponderous

WORDS IN CONTEXT

Based on the context in which each **bold** word is used, identify the word usage of each sentence as either C (Correct) or I (Incorrect).

1. Voracious Victor just picked at mealtimes.

2. Reading and writing are alimentary subjects for any first grade student.

3. The gluttonous guest ate the entire loaf of fresh-baked bread herself.

4. Surviving on celery sticks and rice cakes, Emma became increasingly emaciated.

5. The savory aroma attracted passersby to the new Town Bakery.

Lesson 22

EASY DOES IT
Words Relating to Being Careful

chary circumspect conscientious exacting gingerly heedful
meticulous scrupulous vigilant wary

---

chary *adj.* cautious; wary

Be **chary** about what you say about others. You don't know who may be listening.

Where pickpockets ply their trade, it pays to be **chary** of where you keep your purse or wallet.

Chary of burglars, we set our security alarm whenever we go out.

circumspect *adj.* careful and cautious before acting

Myra is too personally involved in the case to be **circumspect** about it.

Be **circumspect** when choosing a college. Don't get carried away by your emotions.

Kevin contributes less to class discussions than most other students do, but his thoughtful comments reveal his **circumspection**.

conscientious *adj.* relating to doing what one knows is right; scrupulous

Marta was promoted twice for her **conscientious** performance on the job. No one works harder than she does.

You've made a **conscientious** effort to clean the basement, but it's still filthy despite all your hard work.

Tino pumps iron **conscientiously**, at least three times a day for half an hour.

exacting *adj.* requiring a great deal of care or effort; painstaking

The lacrosse coach's standards were so **exacting** that it was hard to achieve them.

It's **exacting** work to build a stereo from a kit. If you are careless, the stereo won't work.

Kyra loves to make tiny pins and brooches, but Kara doesn't have the patience to do such **exacting** work.

gingerly *adj.* very carefully

Because Sue **gingerly** placed the sleeping baby in his crib, the infant didn't wake up.

Build a house of cards **gingerly**. One careless move will make it collapse.

Pet the kitty **gingerly**, or you may hurt it.

heedful *adj.* paying careful attention to

If the novice skier had **heeded** the signs, he wouldn't have found himself on the expert slope.

Be **heedful** of your counselor's advice. His experience is worth a lot when you apply to college.

It's smart to **heed** the instructions before operating a chain saw.

meticulous *adj.* very careful; fussy; finicky; fastidious

A **meticulous** carpenter, Emil makes perfect joints and dovetails, even better than a machine does.

Her makeup is **meticulously** applied. Eyeliner, lipstick, blush—no one puts them on as carefully as Lisa.

During surgery, the incision is kept **meticulously** clean to reduce the possibility of infection.

scrupulous *adj.* showing great care and honesty, based on personal belief of what is right and proper

Jade is **scrupulous** about doing her own work. She won't even let a classmate proofread her papers.

He's as **scrupulous** a politician as you can find anywhere. There's not a hint of scandal in his long career.

Follow the rules of the contest **scrupulously**, or you may be disqualified.

vigilant *adj.* carefully alert and watchful

The driving instructor told his students, "When switching lanes, always look for other cars. **Vigilance** is the price of safety."

Mrs. Trueport **vigilantly** watched the tots playing in the backyard. She didn't take her eyes off them all afternoon.

Ever since Terry fell into a pothole, Dad has been more **vigilant** about keeping the driveway in good repair.

wary *adj.* cautious, careful

If the ship's captain had been more **wary** of storms, he never would have put to sea and lost his boat that day.

Be **wary** of offers that sound too good to be true; they may contain a hidden trap.

We were told to be **wary** of other students who talk even in jest about bringing a gun to school.

MEMORY TIPS

Use these mnemonics (memory devices) to boost your vocabulary. Make up your own memory clues for words in this lesson that are particularly challenging for you. Add these tips—and your own—to your Vocabulary Notebook. Remember, increasing your vocabulary can help you score higher on the verbal section of the SAT I.

chary, wary Learn these two SAT-level synonyms as a rhyming pair— can't get much easier than that!

circumspect This word is a blend of the prefix, *circum-*, and the root, *spec*. *Circum-* means *around* (as in a geometry term you might know, circumference). *Spec* means *seeing* (as in spectator and inspect). In other words, **circumspect** means *looking around*—or being cautious and watchful before making decisions or taking action.

vigilant Write this word in your Vocabulary Notebook, and make the dots of the two *i*'s into "watchful" and "alert" human *eyes*! Once you sketch *eyes* in place of the dots, this memory clue becomes a word-picture clue. Word pictures are very appealing to visual learners, and they tend to stick.

As a noun, a **vigil** is a *night watch*. For example: Since her son had a high fever, the mother kept a **vigil** at his bedside.

wary You know what it means to be a*war*e. Link this preexisting knowledge to **wary**. Both words share the letter cluster *war*. Remember that **wary** and **chary** are SAT I synonyms that sound alike!

MATCHING

Match the vocabulary words in Column A with *one or more* of their defining characteristics appearing in Column B.

Column A	Column B
1. vigilant	a. attentive to detail
2. wary	b. conducting oneself based on a sense of right versus wrong
3. meticulous	c. requiring great effort
4. exacting	d. wide-eyed; alert
5. gingerly	e. very carefully
6. heedful	f. listening to advice or warnings
7. scrupulous	g. fussy
8. circumspect	h. careful, cautious

SAT I-STYLE ANALOGIES

First, express a clear and concise relationship between the two given terms. Next, select the pair in the answer choices that *most closely* shares a similar relationship.

1. RECKLESS : CHARY

   a. vacant : flowing
   b. stained : redone
   c. empty : submissive
   d. dim : bright
   e. globular : strict

2. SCRUPULOUS : MORALITY

   a. great : certification
   b. natural : conversion
   c. healthy : conservation
   d. appreciative : gratitude
   e. exceptional : crispness

3. NIGHT WATCHMAN : VIGILANT

   a. brave : street vendor
   b. ballerina : graceful
   c. conniving : associate
   d. fast : sprinter
   e. grandparent : glib

4. CONSCIENTIOUS : PRINCIPLE

   a. stoic : emotion
   b. competitive : effort
   c. evasive : lucidity
   d. happy : mercy
   e. disgruntled : poise

5. RASH : CIRCUMSPECT

   a. fine : meager
   b. loose : vacant
   c. alarmed : mired
   d. pleased : revealing
   e. cheerful : grim

WORDS IN CONTEXT

Based on the context in which each **bold** word is used, identify the word usage of each sentence as either C (Correct) or I (Incorrect).

1. Wary about her surroundings, Leana always looks over her shoulder when walking the narrow streets of her neighborhood.

2. The circumspect of the three-dimensional figure was hard to measure.

3. Gus's gingerly sense of humor made him the life of every party.

4. A scrupulous and honest handyman, Lee makes sure that every home repair is done efficiently and thoroughly. Client satisfaction is Lee's main goal.

5. Walking across an outdoor tightrope on a windy day is an exacting feat.

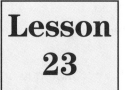

Lesson 23

HERE TODAY, GONE TOMORROW . . .
Words Relating to Being Short-lived in Time or Place

---

ephemeral evanescent fleeting itinerant nomadic peripatetic
transient transitory volatile

---

ephemeral *adj.* lasting a short time; fleeting

Jodi's romances are usually **ephemeral**. She just skips from one boy to another.

Dave has followed baseball steadily since he was nine, but his interest in other sports has been **ephemeral**.

To a child, time goes by slowly, but to an old man, time is **ephemeral**.

evanescent *adj.* vanishing quickly; fleeting

Snowfall in spring is usually **evanescent**. The snow melts very quickly.

The rumor is that an **evanescent** ghost haunts the forest. People who've seen it say that it vanishes as suddenly as it appears.

Old timers tend to lament the **evanescence** of youth. "How quickly youth passes," they say.

fleeting *adj.* short-lived

Willie and Wanda had a **fleeting** romance. Their fling couldn't have lasted more than 24 hours.

Time is **fleeting** when you are enjoying yourself, while pain seems to last forever.

The first sign of trouble was a **fleeting** pain in my stomach that couldn't have lasted for more than a second or two.

itinerant *adj.* wandering about; tending to move around, travel

Susan and Ellie wandered around Europe for months, enjoying a carefree, **itinerant** life.

I rarely see my **itinerant** uncle. He's a globe-hopper, constantly on the move.

Peter's **itinerary** for two weeks included stops in ten cities and five countries.

nomadic *adj.* wandering

Nomadic tribes wandered endlessly around the land.

Oren, like a **nomad**, cannot settle down in one place. He has to keep moving.

Nomadic people who lack permanent homes are often called gypsies.

peripatetic *adj.* moving or walking about; itinerant

During his lecture, the teacher paced **peripatetically** around the room. The constant movement distracted me from what he was saying.

Here today, gone tomorrow. That's the kind of **peripatetic** life Carl enjoys.

Lila was exhausted after a **peripatetic** shopping trip to the city. She had walked from store to store all day long.

transient *adj.* lasting for only a short time; temporary

The motel serves a **transient** clientele. Few visitors stay for more than a night.

The large number of houses up for sale in this neighborhood suggests that the population here is **transient**.

The students are **transients** in a school. They stay for a few years and then leave; the teachers, however, remain in place.

transitory *adj.* fleeting

> On her 100th birthday, Aunt Thalia reflected, "Youth is a **transitory** time of life, while growing old is a more permanent condition."

> The morning fog is **transitory**. It always burns off by midday.

> The joy of winning a game is a **transitory** feeling. It lasts only until the next game.

volatile *adj.* explosive or changing very quickly

> Mia and Greg are a **volatile** couple. One heated argument and their relationship is history.

> Lou can turn angry in an instant. He has a **volatile** temper.

> Careful where you store that can. It contains **volatile** fuel that blows up when heated.

MEMORY TIPS

Use these mnemonics (memory devices) to boost your vocabulary. Make up your own memory clues for words in this lesson that are personally challenging. Add these two tips—and your own—to your Vocabulary Notebook.

evanescent Let the sound of *vanesc*, the underlined part of this word, remind you of *vanishing*, the essential meaning of this SAT word. Again, this memory technique works by linking what you most likely already know (vanishing) to something new (**evanescent**).

transient, transitory Both of these words share the prefix *trans-*, which has to do with movement across. Additional words containing *trans* include transportation, transmit, and translucent.

volatile Because the adjective **volatile** means "explosive; change-able," say "Volatile volcano!" three times in a row. This chant will help to solidify the meaning of the explosive vocabulary word **volatile**. "Volatile volcano! Volatile volcano! Volatile volcano!"

MATCHING

Match the vocabulary words in Column A with *one or more* of their defining characteristics appearing in Column B.

Column A

1. ephemeral
2. transient
3. evanescent
4. volatile
5. peripatetic

Column B

a. explosive
b. traveling about
c. vanishing
d. walking around a lot
e. short-lived

SAT I-STYLE ANALOGIES

First, express a clear and concise relationship between the two given terms. Next, select the pair in the answer choices that *most closely* shares a similar relationship.

1. ROLLING STONE: NOMADIC

    a. teacher's pet : stoic
    b. man's best friend : jumpy
    c. soul mate : beloved
    d. alter ego : triumphant
    e. class clown : vicious

2. TRANSITORY : ENDURING

    a. hearty : latent
    b. zany : clammy
    c. brawny : brainy
    d. overt : covert
    e. legal : impure

3. EVANESCENT : FADING

    a. lithe : partial
    b. tight : light
    c. lax : strict
    d. relaxed : calm
    e. round : orbiting

4. PASSING MOMENT : FLEETING

    a. kind gesture : complementary
    b. false promise : euphemistic
    c. sad occasion : somber
    d. good luck : playful
    e. second chance : reactive

5. TENANT : TRANSIENT

    a. surveyor : feudalistic
    b. meanderer : lethal
    c. messenger : wordy
    d. elder : soft
    e. expert : competent

WORDS IN CONTEXT

Based on the context in which each **bold** word is used, identify the word usage of each sentence as either C (Correct) or I (Incorrect).

1. People who like change prefer a nomadic lifestyle.

2. Sheila's junior year of college was an itinerant one; she traveled to and studied in seven major European cities in nine months.

3. For Jesse, contentment was merely transitory. Unfortunately, he rarely could manage to stay happy for more than 72 hours.

4. A volatile temperament is a highly individualistic one.

5. One might call "momentary lapses of confusion" ephemeral.

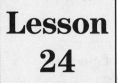

Lesson 24

OLD HAT, NEW HAT?
Words Relating to the Old or the New

antediluvian antiquated antiquity archaic obsolete relic
contemporary inception innovation novel unprecedented

The Old . . .

antediluvian *adj.* very, very old; antiquated

The shop contains **antediluvian** machines that ought to be replaced with up-to-date equipment.

That joke about the chicken crossing the road is **antediluvian**. Can't you think of a more current one?

You can buy that farmhouse for a song because it's **antediluvian**. It even uses gas instead of electricity for lighting.

antiquated *adj.* very old and no longer in use; obsolete

The proverbial housewife standing over a hot stove all day is an **antiquated** stereotype rarely seen anymore.

Some of our history textbooks are **antiquated** and full of outdated information.

The author says he prefers to write on an **antiquated** portable typewriter instead of a computer.

antiquity *n.* ancient times

Antiquity usually refers to times prior to the Middle Ages.

Hippocrates articulated a code of medical ethics as valid today as it was in **antiquity**.

Lord Elgin stole sculptures from sites of **antiquity** in Greece and put them in London's British Museum.

archaic *adj.* old; from a much earlier time; antiquated

Some scholars study **archaic** languages no longer spoken anywhere in the world.

Footnotes are used to explain **archaic** terms known to Shakespeare's audience but not to modern readers.

Some glassmakers use contemporary methods, but most Venetian workshops still rely on **archaic** techniques.

obsolete *adj.* old; outdated, as in no longer in use

My dad has a shelf full of **obsolete** phonograph records containing some of the same music I have on CDs.

In the business world, where everything is stored on computers, filing cabinets full of paper records have become **obsolete**.

Although rotary-dial phones are **obsolete**, our family still uses one for old time's sake.

relic *n.* a custom or object that has been around for a very, very long time

Fritzi's spinning wheel is a **relic** that's been in the family for generations.

The museum displays **relics** of ancient cultures from all over the world.

In some ways Aunt Henrietta seems like a **relic** from the past, but she can quote you the latest rap lyrics verbatim.

The New . . .

contemporary *adj.* modern, new; relating to the same time period

The course is called ***Contemporary*** Civilization, but much of it is devoted to the study of ancient history.

Radiant heat, instead of traditional forced air or steam heat, is becoming the standard in **contemporary** buildings.

Although my art teacher is pretty old, she encourages us to paint in **contemporary** styles.

inception *n.* the start, the beginning of something

Since the **inception** of computers, the library has become a swinging place.

The **inception** of e-mail has cut the cost of postage stamps and envelopes.

The cost of paper has skyrocketed, however, since the **inception** of courses in desktop publishing.

innovation *n.* something new

The coach has instituted an **innovation** in our training. Instead of running ten laps twice a day, he has us running two laps ten times a day.

The company makes **innovative** water filters that can add fresh lemon flavor to tap water.

Gehry's buildings are always **innovative**. No architect has ever designed structures quite like his.

novel *adj.* new

Few other books group vocabulary words according to themes. Barron's believes that the **novel** format of this book will give you an edge when preparing for the SAT I.

Serving kids steamed vegetables for breakfast: now that's a **novel** diet!

A conch shell made into a nightlight is the souvenier shop's best-selling **novelty**.

unprecedented *adj.* novel; unparalleled

The number of delayed flights is **unprecedented**. Never before have so many travelers arrived so late to their destinations.

Giving students money instead of grades for their achievement is **unprecedented** and will never be accepted by the community.

The heat wave this summer is **unprecedented**. There's never been a summer as hot as this one.

MEMORY TIPS

Use these mnemonics (memory devices) to boost your vocabulary. Make up your own memory clues for words in this lesson that are challenging for you. Add these two tips—and your own—to your Vocabulary Notebook.

antiquated, antiquity Like previous memory tips, this one works by linking something you already know to something new. In this case, you most likely know *antique*. Since an *antique* is commonly referred to as something that dates back 100 years or more, link this knowledge to the words **antiquated** and **antiquity**, both having to do with being *very, very* old.

novel, innovation Learn the word root *nova* to help you remember these words and others. *Nova* means *new*. Additional words containing the root *nova* include novice, novelty, and renovate.

Word roots *neo* and *nou* also mean *new*. Words containing these roots include neophyte (beginner, rookie, novice), neonate (newborn), and nouveau riche (a person who has recently become rich).

MATCHING

Match the vocabulary words in Column A with *one or more* of their defining characteristics appearing in Column B.

Column A	Column B
1. relic	a. very, very old
2. obsolete	b. relating to present time
3. novel	c. an invention
4. innovation	d. the very beginning
5. antediluvian	e. a very old object
6. inception	f. outdated; no longer used
7. contemporary	g. original

SAT I-STYLE ANALOGIES

First, express a clear and concise relationship between the two given terms. Next, select the pair in the answer choices that *most closely* shares a similar relationship.

1. PREHISTORIC : CONTEMPORARY
   a. organized : graphic
   b. painted : sealed
   c. loud : boisterous
   d. glittery : dull
   e. vigorous : untied

2. OLD-FASHIONED : OBSOLETE
   a. girdled : lenient
   b. great : junky
   c. zesty : nutty
   d. pointed : dappled
   e. robust : hardy

3. DULL THINKER : INNOVATIVE
   a. monotone speaker : lively
   b. big ego : boastful
   c. old preacher : jesting
   d. young gymnast : jocular
   e. eager beaver : idealistic

4. NOVEL : NOVELTY ITEM
   a. wordy : one-act play
   b. playful : bouncing puppy
   c. underrated : sad legacy
   d. extended : stomachache
   e. reasonable : impossible mission

5. INVENTION : UNPRECEDENTED
   a. formula : encircled
   b. scroll : divided
   c. pin : textured
   d. bucket : empty
   e. thesis : arguable

6. OLD GRECIAN URN : RELIC
   a. gadget : wrench
   b. hair : warmth
   c. tuxedo : attire
   d. disk : track
   e. company : scoreboard

WORDS IN CONTEXT

Based on the context in which each **bold** word is used, determine if the word usage is either C (Correct) or I (Incorrect).

1. Banging coconuts together makes for an antiquated percussive instrument.

2. You could say that contemporary thinkers are "with the times."

3. Jerry adores artwork that has withstood the ages. He frequently shops at "The Inception Connection."

4. Michaelangelo's masterful paintings and sculptures are practically antediluvian, for they have been around since the 16th century.

5. Mrs. Wath is an innovative teacher. She has been using the same teaching methods and supplies for the past 30 years.

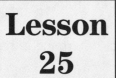

IS ANYBODY THERE? IS ANYTHING THERE?

Words Relating to Being Sneaky or Hardly Noticeable

clandestine covert furtive inconspicuous sly stealthy surreptitious unobtrusive

---

clandestine *adj.* hidden, secret, concealed

During the party, Gia and Jason stole away into the woods for a **clandestine** rendezvous.

It was important to keep the operation **clandestine** to protect our undercover agents.

Hanssen revealed the FBI's **clandestine** plan to build a tunnel under the Russian embassy in Washington.

covert *adj.* secret, hidden

The administration's **covert** plan to overthrow the rebel leader failed because top secret government documents fell into the wrong hands.

Gerry **covertly** transferred funds from the company to his own bank account, but an investigator uncovered Gerry's crime.

Under cover of darkness, the workers slipped **covertly** across the border.

furtive *adj.* sneaky

Jane and Henry didn't know that I observed them exchanging **furtive** glances in biology class.

Knowing that Grandma would disapprove, Robbie **furtively** grabbed a handful of cookies when she wasn't looking.

Before Ben stole a **furtive** peek at Marge's answer sheet, he made sure no one was looking.

inconspicuous *adj.* hardly noticeable

The birthmark on Lilly's cheek was noticeable at birth, but as she grew older it became more and more **inconspicuous**.

Despite her flaming red hair and a figure that usually made heads turn, she remained **inconspicuous** throughout the evening.

Because the bandit made the mistake of wearing a **conspicuous** red hat during the holdup, he was arrested almost immediately.

sly *adj.* underhanded, furtive

Using a **sly** line of questions, Ben tricked the witness into revealing the true story.

All summer Jojo played pool on the **sly**. In September no one realized how skillful he'd become.

At the candy counter, Cal reached for a candy bar and **slyly** stuffed it into his pocket.

stealthy *adj.* secretive, sly

The airplane known as the **Stealth** Bomber lives up to its name by eluding radar detection.

It's the story of a **stealthy** man who breaks into suburban homes but doesn't steal anything. He just gets his kicks that way.

Using **stealth**, the Navy Seals avoided detection and blew up the enemy ship.

surreptitious *adj.* done or made in a secret, stealthy way

Using **surreptitious** methods, the terrorists planted a time bomb in the railway station. Fortunately the device was found before it could explode.

William's **surreptitious** behavior has me worried. He's up to something sneaky, I'm sure.

During the test, Damian **surreptitiously** studied the answer sheet he had taped to the palm of his hand.

unobtrusive *adj.* inconspicuous; not easily noticed

There was nothing **unobtrusive** about Tina's diamond earrings; they were the size of golf balls.

Sophie hates being noticed, so she wears the most **unobtrusive** clothes imaginable.

The table stood **unobtrusively** in the corner for years until Aunt Rhoda noticed it was a valuable antique.

MEMORY TIPS

Use these mnemonics (memory devices) to boost your vocabulary. Make up your own memory clues for words in this lesson that are personally challenging. Add these two tips—and your own—to your Vocabulary Notebook. Vocabulary is at the heart of this test.

covert Think *covered* when you see this word. As the definition tells you, **covert** means *hidden* or *secret*. Now certainly *covered* relates to this word's definition. In fact, in some sentences the contextual meaning of **covert** could simply mean *covered*.

inconspicuous It is helpful to know the root word *spic* (also *spec*) in order to commit this word to your memory. *Spic* has to do with *seeing*. (Think of these words: spectacle, spectator, inspect). As you might already know, the prefix *con-* (and *com-*) means *with* or *together*. In this particular word, the first prefix in this word, *in-*, means *not*. So, linking the prefixes and roots together, **inconspicuous** more or less means "not with seeing." There you have it; **inconspicuous** means *hardly noticeable*.

SAT I-STYLE ANALOGIES

First, express a clear and concise relationship between the two given terms. Next, select the pair in the answer choices that *most closely* shares a similar relationship.

1. OVERT : COVERT

   a. extroverted : introverted
   b. mild : moderate
   c. wild : headstrong
   d. nifty : meek
   e. urban : mediocre

2. FURTIVE : EXPOSED

   a. lean : rugged
   b. credible : internal
   c. sporty : athletic
   d. arranged : haphazard
   e. prepaid : increased

3. FOX : SLY

   a. panther : hungry
   b. moose : loathsome
   c. ape : docile
   d. tortoise : slow
   e. hyena : icy

4. STEALTHY : PRIVATE INVESTIGATOR

   a. inflected : singer
   b. formidable : flutist
   c. regular : boy
   d. pious : reverend
   e. variable : chief

5. SKYSCRAPER : UNOBTRUSIVE

   a. landmark : lengthy
   b. statue : marbleized
   c. railroad : automated
   d. mall : expensive
   e. glass : opaque

WORDS IN CONTEXT

Based on the context in which each **bold** word is used, identify the word usage of each sentence as either C (Correct) or I (Incorrect).

1. **Covert** activities are public knowledge.

2. Wearing an oversized hat and with long hair hanging over her face, Dawn was obviously trying to make herself **inconspicuous**.

3. Luke **furtively** made his phone calls to Jessica since he knew his parents did not approve of his latest girlfriend.

4. A **sly** trick is one that all are meant to understand.

5. Janet and Mark kept their hand-holding **clandestine** since they wanted the world to know their affection for one another.

Review Exercises / Lessons 21–25

NAME THAT CLUSTER

To the left of the groups of words, put the Roman numeral that corresponds with these theme (or cluster) titles:

Words Relating to . . .

I. Being Careful
II. The Old or the New
III. Food and Hunger
IV. Being Sneaky or Hardly Noticeable
V. Short-lived in Time or Place

Cluster Title _____   1. sly, surreptitious, stealthy, inconspicuous, unobtrusive

Cluster Title _____   2. archaic, novel, innovative, antediluvian, obsolete

Cluster Title _____   3. voracious, alimentary, savory, palatable, emaciated

Cluster Title _____   4. transient, peripatetic, nomadic, itinerant, ephemeral

Cluster Title _____   5. chary, conscientious, heedful, scrupulous, wary

SENTENCE COMPLETIONS

Read the sentence through carefully. Then from the five vocabulary words given in parentheses, circle the word that fits *best*.

1. In the past five years, the Delsons have lived in the United States, Switzerland, and England. They are truly a (an) _____ family. (innovative, covert, transient, heedful, arcane)

2. At _____ school, Mia learned how to prepare the perfect omelet and bake the perfect chocolate mousse cake. (itinerant, gluttony, furtive, culinary, unprecedented)

3. Only three buckets of popcorn and two grilled cheese sandwiches could satisfy Meyers's _____ appetite.
(nomadic, epicurean, fleeting, clandestine, gluttonous)

4. Gunther was a _____ employee who was the first person in and the last to leave every day.
(conscientious, emaciated, innovative, surreptitious, delectable)

5. For most people, liver and onions are not very _____.
(abstemious, meticulous, furtive, evanescent, palatable)

6. A (An) _____ undercover agent, Roy tried to remain _____ no matter where he went.
contemporary...stealthy
clandestine...unprecedented
surreptitious...covert
archaic...stealthy
conspicuous...clandestine

7. It's virtually impossible for a bedazzling _____ like fireworks to be _____.
relic...sly
furtive...obtrusive
inception...stealthy
antiquity...surreptitious
spectacle...inconspicuous

ONE DOESN'T BELONG

Three of the words in each grouping relate to each other somehow. Cross off the one word that does not belong with the others. For a challenge, write the word that does not belong on the line below, and try your best to define that word. *Note:* Some of the words have been taken from definitions or exercises that appear within the lessons.

1. savory   sly   surreptitious   stealthy

_____ means _____

2. peripatetic   itinerant   fleeting   furtive

_____ means _____

3. unprecedented   unparalleled   novel   antediluvian

_____ means _____

4. delectable   evanescent   culinary   epicurean

_____ means _____

5. painstaking   exacting   meticulous   obsolete

_____ means _____

DO YOU KNOW THESE PEOPLE?

Words Relating to People You Will Meet on the SAT I

adversary advocate artisan ascetic charlatan hedonist orator pariah raconteur skeptic virtuoso

---

adversary *n.* an opponent

To Wanda's frustration, her math teacher seemed more like an **adversary** than a guide through the mysteries of calculus.

Jay and Ken were long-time friends and colleagues, but their disagreement turned them into **adversaries**.

Off the court they are pals, but on the court they play tennis like the staunchest **adversaries**.

advocate *n.* a supporter; proponent

As an **advocate** for children, Millie spends her days trying to eradicate all forms of child abuse, neglect, and maltreatment.

My best friend Laura is my eternal **advocate**; she will support me vociferously for the rest of my life.

Are you an **advocate** for increased spending or decreased funding when it comes to preserving the environment?

artisan *n.* a person who is skillful with his or her hands

In Italy, my grandfather worked as an **artisan**, more specifically as a glassblower.

A group of **artisans** was hired to build a charming stone wall around the property.

Every weekend **artisans** display and sell their crafts on the village green.

ascetic *n.* a person who refrains from indulging in earthly pleasures

Tiffany lives **ascetically**. Her home is a simple one-room cabin in the woods.

The ascetic gave away all his possessions and went to Central America, where he worked as a missionary.

Why would one who claims to be an **ascetic** own five wristwatches and a suitcase full of jewelry?

charlatan *n.* a fraud; a quack or imposter

The new biology teacher was a **charlatan**. His college degree was actually in comparative literature.

The book is about a **charlatan**, an uneducated imposter who pretended to be a physician.

Is the minister someone we can trust and believe in, or is he merely a **charlatan**?

hedonist *n.* a person who lives for pleasure

Michael is too much of a **hedonist** to get a job. He'd rather just play around.

We lived like **hedonists** during our vacation at Club Med. For a week we frolicked on the beach, danced all night, and had nothing but great food and fun.

Her **hedonistic** lifestyle soon grew boring, so Heidi went back to school and to work.

orator *n.* a skillful public speaker

Martin Luther King's speech, "I Have a Dream," established him as one of the best **orators** of all time.

An acclaimed **orator**, Oliver captivates his audience with his voice inflection, choice of words, and poignant use of figurative language.

The **orator** received a standing ovation for his outstanding oration. (Try repeating that three times!)

pariah *n.* a social outcast

After he painted his house bright orange, Paul became the neighborhood **pariah**. No one on the block wanted anything to do with him.

Hilda is a **pariah**, but she doesn't mind being an outcast because she has poetry to keep her company.

After the scandal, Shoeless Joe became a **pariah**. Expelled from the game, he never played baseball again.

raconteur *n.* a skillful storyteller

Uncle Stephan is our family **raconteur**. He has endless stories to tell about life in the old country.

Rod is a creative **raconteur**. He can make up a story based on the simplest everyday occurrence.

Mr. Stanley should be more of a teacher and less of a **raconteur**. I'm sick of hearing his stories about the Navy.

skeptic *n.* a person who doubts

Now do you believe in UFOs, or are you still a **skeptic**?

Many **skeptics** still don't accept the conclusions of the Warren Commission.

Mary is **skeptical** about the wisdom of buying on credit, so she pays for everything in cash.

virtuoso *n.* a highly skilled performer, usually a musical performer

Ellen gave a **virtuoso** performance on the court, scoring 60 points and grabbing 24 rebounds.

As a **virtuoso** trumpeter, Danny stands a good chance of getting into the Juilliard School.

Since age 6, Sarah has been a **virtuoso** with a violin. At age 12, she started making recordings and performing in concert halls worldwide.

MEMORY TIPS

Use these mnemonics (memory devices) to boost your vocabulary. Make up your own memory clues for words in this lesson that are personally challenging. Add these two tips—and your own—to your Vocabulary Notebook. Remember, vocabulary building is key to increasing your score on the verbal SAT I.

virtuoso Let the *vi* remind you of <u>vi</u>olin. Now imagine a highly skilled violinist playing classical music. In other words, picture a **virtuoso** performing on stage in your mind's eye.

raconteur Do you know what it means to *recount* a story? *Recount* is an infinitive verb that means "to tell or to narrate." So you see, a **raconteur** is one who tells stories well.

MATCHING

Match the vocabulary words in Column A with *one or more* of their defining characteristics appearing in Column B.

Column A	Column B
1. charlatan ℮	a. a doubter
2. raconteur ♭	b. a storyteller
3. ascetic ♢	c. a speech maker
4. skeptic ↖	d. a self-denying individual
5. orator ↺	e. an imposter
6. advocate ↑	f. a supporter

SAT I-STYLE ANALOGIES

First, express a clear and concise relationship between the two given terms. Next, select the pair in the answer choices that *most closely* shares a similar relationship.

1. ORATOR : SPEAKER

   a. gymnast : toddler
   b. painter : artist
   c. virtuoso : musician
   d. writer : composer
   e. trickster : magician

2. QUALMS : SKEPTIC

   a. reveries : daydreamer
   b. longings : gymnast
   c. whispers : vocalist
   d. grunts : mind reader
   e. follies : player

3. FOE : ADVERSARY

    a. doll : woman
    b. screamer : leader
    c. legend : creature
    d. ballerina : pianist
    e. boss : leader

4. ASCETIC : HEDONIST

    a. challenger : contender
    b. jumper : panderer
    c. extrovert : introvert
    d. victim : avenger
    e. populist : soldier

5. OSTRACIZE : PARIAH

    a. vilify : umpire
    b. pledge : tattletale
    c. uplift : bully
    d. avoid : troublemaker
    e. validate : insomniac

6. ARTISAN : HANDICRAFT

    a. gourmand : restaurant
    b. officer : jail
    c. baker : pastry
    d. dentist : drill
    e. scalpel : surgeon

7. ORATOR : PULPIT

    a. cowboy : field
    b. dilettante : library
    c. clown : circus tent
    d. bungler : party
    e. stockbroker : newsroom

WORDS IN CONTEXT

Based on the context in which each **bold** word is used, identify the word usage of each sentence as either C (Correct) or I (Incorrect).

1. The masterful advocate prepared decadent desserts.

2. Playing three sports well makes one an accomplished virtuoso.

3. Bruce, a hedonist at heart, gives in to his every whim and desire.

4. Living among charlatans can make one doubt humankind's authenticity.

5. Silversmiths were widespread artisans during America's colonial times.

Lesson 27

IT JUST DOESN'T MATTER

Words Relating to Things of Little Importance or Value

> **extraneous frivolous incidental inconsequential irrelevant
> negligible peripheral petty superficial trifling trivial**

extraneous *adj.* not necessary; not an essential part; not relevant

In your oral report, include only the highlights of your paper. Leave out all **extraneous** matters.

The detective scrutinized the crime scene, taking note of everything, even the most **extraneous** details.

Let's stick to the heart of the matter and put your **extraneous** concerns aside for the moment.

frivolous *adj.* not having substance or a sense of importance or seriousness; silly; trivial; trifling

Lenny sued the chef because there was a dead fly in his soup, but the judge threw out the complaint on grounds that it was **frivolous**.

Forget about looking for a deep meaning in that story. It's totally **frivolous**.

If you ask a silly question, you deserve a **frivolous** response.

incidental *adj.* less important; minor

An **incidental** benefit of not having your own car is that you walk a lot and get plenty of exercise.

In college, tuition, room, and board make up the bulk of the cost, but there are numerous **incidental** expenses, too.

While studying the scratch on my car, I noticed **incidentally** that I needed air in this tire.

inconsequential *adj.* irrelevant; of no significance; unimportant

The collision produced a huge sound, but the damage to the cars was **inconsequential**.

During the term Malcolm failed one quiz, but the impact on his final grade was **inconsequential**.

It's **inconsequential** whether Jean studies math for an hour or for a week. She still earns A's.

irrelevant *adj.* not relating to the matter at hand

That Marnie has a cold is **irrelevant** to her cutting classes.

The teacher said that since the essay was awful, the amount of time I spent writing it is **irrelevant** to the grade.

Ron tried to hide the truth with a smokescreen of **irrelevancies**.

negligible *adj.* able or likely to be neglected or bypassed due to small-ness or lack of importance

Unfortunately, the patient made **negligible** improvement overnight.

Peter refused the job offer because the increase in salary was **negligible**.

Although the tire looked flat, it took only a **negligible** amount of air.

peripheral *adj.* only marginally connected to what is truly important; minor or incidental; relating to the field of vision

The class discussion got bogged down in **peripheral** matters that had nothing to do with the issue of cloning.

What's important to me is the salary. Benefits and everything else are **peripheral**.

Deer have excellent **peripheral** vision. They can see movement in all directions except right behind them.

petty *adj.* minor or trivial; small in quantity; paltry

Igor complained about some **petty** flaws, like lint on the clothing and a wrinkled bedsheet.

Their arguments were about **petty** matters. There was no big issue between them.

The messenger was fired because of the **petty** complaints of his supervisor.

superficial *adj.* lacking in depth or importance; on the surface

The paper received a poor grade because I didn't go deeply into Hawthorne's writing. The teacher said I dealt with it **superficially**.

The wound was **superficial**. It was only skin deep and hardly bled at all.

I hate the **superficial** conversations that I'm forced into at my parents' parties.

trifling *adj.* lacking significance; unimportant

In the long run, cutting down one tree may seem **trifling**, but once the precedent is set, the whole forest may be cut down.

"Lying during your college interview is no **trifling** matter," said Mother. "In fact, it could cause you to be rejected."

He called after midnight with some **trifling** news that could easily have waited until morning.

trivial *adj.* unimportant; trifling; ordinary

Because rain is needed badly, the **trivial** amount that fell yesterday is not going to ease the drought.

So much of the class was taken up by **trivialities** that hardly any time was left to discuss important matters.

Gordy is a world-class expert in hockey **trivia**. Ask him anything about pro hockey, and he'll know the answer.

MEMORY TIPS

Use these mnemonics (memory devices) to boost your vocabulary. Make up your own memory clues for words in this lesson that are personally challenging. Add these two tips—and your own—to your Vocabulary Notebook. Remember, vocabulary building is key to increasing your score on the verbal SAT I.

petty Learn **petty** along with the word *paltry* (unimportant, small). After all, they share three consonants (p, t, y), they start and end with the same letter, and they each have two syllables. *Petty* and **paltry** are an SAT I synonym pair. Write them together in your Vocabulary Notebook.

superficial For this word, knowing the prefix *super-* (*above*) is extremely helpful. Superman is *above* other men because of his above-normal strength and power. In addition, notice that the word *surface* can be spelled using the letters found in **superficial**. A **superficial** understanding, then, reaches only the surface and lacks depth.

MATCHING

Match the vocabulary words in Column A with *one or more* of their defining characteristics appearing in Column B.

Column A	Column B
1. superficial *c*	a. unimportant
2. trivial *a, d*	b. only slightly related
3. extraneous *b, a*	c. shallow; lacking depth
4. trifling *a, d*	d. insignificant
5. frivolous *e*	e. not very serious

SAT I-STYLE ANALOGIES

First, express a clear and concise relationship between the two given terms. Next, select the pair in the answer choices that *most closely* shares a similar relationship.

1. TRIFLING : MAJOR

   a. zany : lighthearted
   b. united : divided
   c. impractical : impetuous
   d. stimulating : predominant
   e. grumpy : necessary

2. JAUNTY : FRIVOLOUS

   a. bumpy : jumpy
   b. glandular : spunky
   c. slippery : rugged
   d. thriving : flourishing
   e. communal : rugged

3. PETTY : TRIVIA

   a. late : doubts
   b. sour : lemons
   c. secretive : keys
   d. crunchy : bonbons
   e. vaulted : machines

4. TRIFLING : FRIVOLOUS

   a. arduous : demanding
   b. gleaming : alighting
   c. mistreated : limping
   d. backhanded : trailing
   e. remorseless : careening

5. FAIR-WEATHER FRIENDS : SUPERFICIAL

   a. strict lieutenants : bewitching
   b. unruly motorists : perilous
   c. dreamy astronomers : elevating
   d. strong titans : languorous
   e. nimble puppeteers : flighty

WORDS IN CONTEXT

Based on the context in which each **bold** word is used, identify the word usage of each sentence as either C (Correct) or I (Incorrect).

1. The number of possessions one owns is **trivial** when compared to the number of close family members and friends one has.

2. The association members were disappointed by the **superficiality** of the speaker's topics for discussion.

3. **Frivolous** protests will receive priority status.

4. Despite their **petty** dimes and nickels, the lemonade stand operators were thrilled with their piggy bank stash.

5. Eager to become a world-renowned actor, the young starlet never passed on a stage role, no matter how small or **trifling**.

LIKE AN OWL

Words Relating to Being Wise and Sharp-Minded

acute astute discerning erudite incisive ingenious judicious perspicacious prudent sagacious savvy shrewd

acute *adj.* keen-minded; sharp

Because it supposedly improves mental **acuity**, fish is called brain food.

Natalie's **acute** intellect contrasts with the dull minds of her classmates.

Dee had a dull ache in her tooth, but this morning the pain was much more **acute**.

astute *adj.* sharp-minded; very clever

The teacher said, "How **astute** you must be to have found that mistake in the problem. No one has ever noticed it before."

An **astute** lawyer, Jonah wins most of his cases.

As an **astute** reader of poetry, Helen seems always to find meanings hidden between the lines.

discerning *adj.* able to judge people and situations clearly

The **discerning** audience easily detected the sarcasm in the comedian's jokes.

As a **discerning** collector, Harry buys only the very best bluegrass recordings on the market.

If you look carefully, you may **discern** a small boat out there in the fog.

erudite *adj.* wise due to much reading and studying; scholarly

Mr. Major seems like a plain, simple guy, but he is **erudite** and a well-respected scholar of ancient languages.

Morris pretends to be **erudite**, but he's really an airhead.

He attributes his **erudition** to a lifetime of studying and reading good books.

incisive *adj.* sharp; keen

Brian's **incisive** comments went right to the heart of the matter.

It took many **incisive** minds to figure out the structure of the genome.

No one ever accused Mortimer of having an **incisive** wit. He's as dull as they come.

ingenious *adj.* very clever or inventive

The Osprey, an aircraft that lands like a helicopter but flies like a plane, is an **ingenious** invention, but it has had numerous technical problems.

Ingenious it may be, but a digital belt buckle is a pretty useless item.

Claude came up with an **ingenious** alternative to the broken computer: a piece of paper and a pencil.

judicious *adj.* showing wisdom in judging people and situations

By keeping to a budget, Marlene makes **judicious** use of her limited income.

Since you get only one guess, think about it **judiciously** beforehand.

Henny chose a college without thinking much about it, but Nora is trying to be more **judicious**.

perspicacious *adj.* using wise judgment; sharp-minded

As a **perspicacious** observer of teenagers, Mr. Krystal knew instantly that Kenny had a problem.

The most **perspicacious** scene in the play is the family dinner. Donna captured a typical dinnertime conversation exactly.

Dana can do a **perspicacious** impersonation of the president's speech, gestures, and facial expressions.

prudent *adj.* careful, cautious, and wise

It is **prudent** not to drive when the roads are covered with ice.

Because he was tired and sleepy, Charles made a **prudent** decision to stop for coffee.

Before agreeing to buy an old house, it would be **prudent** to have the place checked for termites.

sagacious *adj.* wise

For a three-year old, my kid brother says the most **sagacious** things. Unlike me, he may be a budding genius.

Ms. Roth wrote, "This **sagacious** essay is full of impressive insights." From her, that's quite a compliment.

As a **sagacious** observer, Agee was able to recreate just what it was like on a typical summer morning in Knoxville.

savvy *adj.* smart; informed

The salesman tried to hide the car's defects, but Will was **savvy** enough to find them.

Samantha is **savvy** enough to find her way around San Francisco without a map.

Savvy investors knew better than to put their money in Vince's risky business venture.

shrewd *adj.* insightful; clever

Dennis is **shrewd** enough not to be deceived by the fast-talking used car salesman.

Marion is a **shrewd** negotiator, always getting the deal she wants but leaving the other side pleased with the outcome.

Jonas scored after faking out the defense with a **shrewd** move up the middle of the field.

MEMORY TIPS

acute As you probably know from your math studies, **acute** angles are those that are less than 90 degrees. In other words, **acute** angles are *sharp*—sharper than obtuse (blunt) angles. So, link *sharp angles* to *sharp-minded* people.

Note: Obtuse means dim-witted.

judicious Let the *jud* at the beginning of this word make you think of *judge*. Now I'm sure you agree that a judge ought to be **judicious** (sensible and wise when it comes to "judging" people and their circumstances, for example). Do not confuse **judicious** with judgmental; the latter term has to do with criticizing, finding fault.

perspicacious You can build the meaning of this word by knowing the meaning of its prefix and root. The prefix *peri-* means "around." The root *spic* (also *spec* as in spectator or inspect) has to do with "looking or seeing." So, **perspicacious** has to do with "looking and seeing all around." If one is **perspicacious**, then one is also perceptive—able to clearly see through and around.

MATCHING

Match the vocabulary words in Column A with *one or more* of their defining characteristics appearing in Column B.

Column A

1. sagacious c, d
2. prudent c, d
3. perspicacious a
4. acute b
5. ingenious e

Column B

a. showing good judgment
b. sharp
c. like a sage or wise elder
d. perceptive
e. imaginative

SAT I-STYLE ANALOGIES

First, express a clear and concise relationship between the two given terms. Next, select the pair in the answer choices that *most closely* shares a similar relationship.

1. ACUTE : BLUNT

    a. new : grim
    b. wan : colorful
    c. dire : mint
    d. vivid : pallid
    e. stiff : minced

2. ORIGINATOR : INGENIOUS

    a. flame eater : daring
    b. yogi : mirthful
    c. attorney : gentle
    d. altar boy : dirigible
    e. surveyor : direful

3. JUDICIOUS : FAIRNESS

    a. pliable : stiffness
    b. tactful : finesse
    c. doleful : allegiance
    d. loyal : alacrity
    e. vehement : realism

4. SHREWD : WISE PERSON

    a. boring : lector
    b. fidgety : youth
    c. tasteful : homeowner
    d. egotistical : braggart
    e. limp : actuary

5. PRAGMATIC : PRACTICAL

    a. bold : audacious
    b. unnerving : waning
    c. truculent : longwinded
    d. outrageous : prim
    e. elitist : well-groomed

WORDS IN CONTEXT

Based on the context in which each **bold** word is used, identify the word usage of each sentence as either C (Correct) or I (Incorrect).

1. Building a new kind of doghouse might be the undertaking of an **ingenious** individual.

2. **Prudent** investing involves the random selection of stocks and mutual funds.

3. "Very **sagacious**, Myrtle. You knew just what the Grubers were thinking."

4. An **incisive** mentality understands issues and circumstances on a surface level.

5. In addition to many other aspects of language phenomena, shades of meaning and slang are studied by the **incisive** linguist.

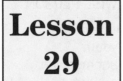

Lesson 29

TRICKY TWINS AND TRIPLETS

Words That Sound and/or Look Alike But Have Different Meanings

acrid/arid aesthetic/ascetic/atheistic ambiguous/ambivalent
coalesce/convalesce delusion/allusion/illusion

---

acrid *adj.* bitter, harsh

Acrid exhaust fumes from the traffic inside the tunnel made him cough.

The comedian's **acrid** humor rubs salt into many wounds.

The **acrid** smell inside the room made me gag.

arid *adj.* dry, lacking water

On one side of the island it rains all the time; the other side is totally **arid**.

The arroyo once had running water in it, but now is **arid**.

Arid air inside the plane dries my skin.

aesthetic *adj.* having to do with artistic beauty

To build a house that ugly shows a lack of **aesthetic** taste.

Bertha gets her sense of **aesthetics** from her mother, who is a successful artist and designer.

There is something **aesthetically** wrong with that painting. It pushes you away instead of drawing you in.

ascetic (from Lesson 26) *n.* a person who refrains from indulging in earthly pleasures

Tiffany lives like an **ascetic**. Her home is a simple one-room cabin in the woods.

The **ascetic** gave away all his possessions and went to Central America, where he worked as a missionary.

Why would one who claims to be an **ascetic** own five wristwatches and a suitcase full of jewelry?

atheistic *adj.* without a belief in any god

Although James was raised as a strict Catholic, he became an **atheist** in college.

Although they don't believe in God, **atheists** can still experience spirituality.

Henry tried to convince his **atheistic** brother that God exists.

ambiguous *adj.* hard to understand; unclear; open to more than one interpretation

Because Hester's answer was totally **ambiguous**, I don't know whether she agrees or disagrees.

By leaving the passage **ambiguous**, the author wants the reader to decide what it means.

People who prefer definite answers are often uncomfortable with **ambiguity**.

ambivalent *adj.* having conflicting feelings or opinions about something; unsure

Rose feels **ambivalent** about the weekend in Vermont. She wants to go, but she also wants to stay at home.

Ambivalence paralyzes Penny; she can't make up her mind about anything.

If you expect to win the argument, be confident that you are right. **Ambivalence** will be taken as a sign of weakness.

coalesce *vb.* to have different opinions join together; fuse; converge

By the end of the meeting, the various viewpoints somehow **coalesced** into a coherent policy.

The legislators **coalesced** behind Senator Cooke and elected her unanimously.

Gravity forced billions of atoms to **coalesce** into a single lump of rock.

convalesce *vb.* to recover from an illness

After her hip surgery, Grandma **convalesced** at home instead of in the hospital.

A **convalescence** of two months kept Joe from his job.

While **convalescing** from a leg wound, Lt. Henry fell in love with his nurse.

delusion *n.* a false opinion or belief

To expect to get into Yale with an 880 College Board score is nothing but a **delusion**.

"It might be self-**delusion** or wishful thinking, but I think that Barry has fallen in love with me," said Brenda.

The story tells of a lowly clerk who has **deluded** himself into thinking he's the king of Spain.

allusion *n.* an indirect reference, often to literature

The book is hard to read unless you understand the author's **allusions** to Greek and Roman mythology.

Carla interpreted the poet's reference to "hound dog" as an **allusion** to Elvis.

It's as though Mr. Hargrove is living in the past. He always **alludes** to the 1960s when he wants to make a point.

illusion *n.* something unreal that gives the appearance of being real

If you expect to pass this course after failing every quiz and test, you are living an **illusion**.

Although he can barely draw a straight line, Morris developed the **illusion** that he is a great artist.

My favorite magic trick is the **illusion** of turning a cup of coffee into a cup full of shiny pennies.

MEMORY TIPS

Use these mnemonics (memory devices) to boost your vocabulary. Make up your own memory clues for words in this lesson that are personally challenging. Add these two tips—and your own—to your Vocabulary Notebook.

ambiguous, ambivalent As a prefix, *ambi-* means *both*. If you didn't know this prefix, then you might have known *bi-*, meaning *two*. In either case, the idea of *both* or *two* is behind the meanings of these vocabulary words. To review, the first listed means "having two (or more) meanings"; the second, "having two conflicting feelings about something or someone." Ambidexterous means being able to use your left and right hands skillfully.

arid Have you heard of the antiperspirant, Arid? Well, the commercials tell us that Arid keeps you "extra dry." Who says television isn't educational?

MATCHING

Match the vocabulary words in Column A with *one or more* of their defining characteristics appearing in Column B.

Column A	Column B
1. illusion	a. denying oneself pleasure
2. convalesce	b. harsh, biting
3. allusion	c. a reference
4. ascetic	d. a magic trick
5. acrid	e. to get well again

SAT I-STYLE ANALOGIES

First, express a clear and concise relationship between the two given terms. Next, select the pair in the answer choices that *most closely* shares a similar relationship.

1. DIVERGENT : COALESCE

    a. hanging : collide
    b. jumpy : calm
    c. vivacious : negate
    d. disparate : converge
    e. engaged : beam

2. AESTHETE : AESTHETIC

    a. linguist : neurotic
    b. imp : mischievous
    c. theorist : lucky
    d. coachman : sidetracked
    e. wisecracker : demonic

3. ARID : BONE DRY

    a. smart : sharp
    b. fine : rustic
    c. tasty : sweet
    d. pretty : gorgeous
    e. lackluster : dull

4. DOCTOR : CONVALESCE

    a. emcee : research
    b. heartthrob : idealize
    c. vegetarian : economize
    d. chauffeur : soliloquize
    e. tour guide : sightsee

5. ILLUSION : HALLUCINATION

    a. vitamin : eggplant
    b. pant : boot-cut
    c. drum : rattle
    d. Caesar : Roman
    e. laptop : bucket

WORDS IN CONTEXT

Based on the context in which each **bold** word is used, identify the word usage of each sentence as either C (Correct) or I (Incorrect).

1. As an ascetic, Edgar prefers to live in a dry climate.

2. The delusions that Mario the Great Magician performed on stage played with Sabrina's mind for days after the show.

3. When opinions coalesce, conflicts eventually subside.

4. People who regularly go to museums and art galleries have strong aesthetic interests.

5. Acrid rumors can sometimes hurt an individual as much as physical pain.

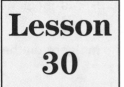

Lesson 30 — MORE TRICKY TWINS AND TRIPLETS

imprudent *adj.* careless; rash

Quitting her job in a moment of anger proved to be **imprudent**; Lindsay would not be able to save enough money to attend her own senior prom.

Jogging at night without wearing reflective clothing is **imprudent**.

It is **imprudent** to wait until the last minute to register for classes. All the good classes fill up quickly.

impudent *adj.* rude; disrespectful

Answering my father in an **impudent** manner guaranteed that I would lose car privileges for at least a week.

The teacher decided she had had enough of the class's **impudent** behavior and gave them all detention.

The group of kids sitting in the back of the movie theater was so loud and **impudent** that the usher made them leave.

indigenous *adj.* native

Eucalyptus trees grow all over the world, but they are **indigenous** to Australia.

Indigenous people in the United States are called Native Americans.

Pineapples are **indigenous** to Hawaii.

indigent *adj.* poor; impoverished

Angela's Ashes is the story of an **indigent** family living hand-to-mouth in the slums of Limerick, Ireland.

As a lawyer for the Legal Aid Society, Martin represents **indigent** clients in court.

The movie is about a middle-class girl who winds up **indigent** on the streets of Chicago.

indignant *adj.* angry

Mr. Jason became **indignant** when Jake interrupted the performance by asking to go to the bathroom.

Billy's insulting and crude remarks left Mama upset and **indignant**.

What makes me most **indignant** is someone cutting in line ahead of me.

intimate *vb.* to suggest; to hint at

My college advisor **intimated** that if I kept my grades up I might qualify for a scholarship.

When Jennifer told Mike that he looked slim, Mike replied, "Are you **intimating** that I used to look fat?"

The principal **intimated** that school might be closed if heavy snow is predicted.

intimidate *vb.* to frighten; to hint at

At 6 feet 4 inches tall and 240 pounds, Ben easily **intimidates** little kids just by glaring at them.

Now that she has mastered kung fu, Cherri is no longer **intimidated** when she crosses the campus alone at night.

Marcy is **intimidated** by standardized tests, but she is learning to deal with her fears.

obscure *adj.* hard to understand; abstract

The point of the story is a little **obscure**, but the characters are crystal clear.

Maria found an allusion to an **obscure** monk in 14th-century Italy who invented what we now call a pencil.

Tom started as an **obscure** actor in the provinces, but now he's world famous.

obtuse *adj.* stupid; not clear or precise

Are you being deliberately **obtuse** or are you just naturally stupid?

I hate to appear **obtuse**, but I just don't understand quadratic equations.

Even after remarking on the out-of-state license plates, the officer still asked **obtuse** questions about whether I was a resident of the state.

ponderable *adj.* important enough to require a lot of thought

Whether to skip classes to take a driving test is an easy question for some people, but for Cynthia it's a **ponderable** dilemma.

It's a **ponderable** issue whether to break up with Keith before the prom or after the prom.

Dad said, "I don't have time for a **ponderable** question on the meaning of life just now. Let's discuss it over dinner, okay?"

ponderous *adj.* very heavy or bulky; dull or lifeless

Willa Cather's style of writing is **ponderous** to read. I prefer something more energetic and lively.

It's hard to believe how the filmmaker turned an exciting adventure story into a dark, **ponderous** tale of jealousy and betrayal.

It's a slow, **ponderous** novel about a poor fisherman and his net. It was supposed to be deep, but the meaning escaped me.

MEMORY TIPS

Use these mnemonics (memory devices) to boost your vocabulary. Make up your own memory clues for words in this lesson that are challenging for you. Add these three tips—and your own—to your Vocabulary Notebook.

indigent This clue will not help you distinguish **indigent** from its tricky triplets, yet this clue will help you remember this word on its own. Let the *indi* at the beginning remind you of India, which is a Third-World country that suffers from substantial poverty. Again, be alert to words that might cause confusion since they look or sound similar to this word. In other words, remember the different meanings of indigent, indigenous, and indignant.

intimate When you say this word aloud for practice, add an "h" sound to the beginning to get *(h)intimate*. If you say the word so many times in that way, it should stick. So from now on, think *(h)intimate*.

obtuse Chances are you know that obtuse angles are greater than 90 degrees, right? So, what kind of "point" is formed by an obtuse angle? A blunt one. That's right, **obtuse** means *blunt*, as in blunt-minded, not-so-sharp, or simply stupid. Remember not to confuse this word with *obscure*.

MATCHING

Match the vocabulary words in Column A with *one or more* of their defining characteristics appearing in Column B.

Column A	Column B
1. indigenous	a. angry
2. obscure	b. bulky to carry
3. indignant	c. hard to understand
4. ponderous	d. hint at
5. ponderable	e. requiring a lot of thought
6. intimate	f. native
7. intimidate	g. to frighten

SAT I-STYLE ANALOGIES

First, express a clear and concise relationship between the two given terms. Next, select the pair in the answer choices that *most closely* shares a similar relationship.

1. INTIMATE : INSINUATE

   a. enlarge : reduce
   b. block : number
   c. copy : carve
   d. certify : title
   e. customize : personalize

2. MILLIONAIRE : INDIGENT

   a. mechanic : lopsided
   b. batter : stunted
   c. big mouth : mute
   d. surfer : liquid
   e. debtor : prevalent

3. IMPUDENT : IMP

   a. unyielding : newborn
   b. childish : assessor
   c. assiduous : claimant
   d. elevated : attendant
   e. lifeless : corpse

4. APPARENT : OBSCURE

   a. platinum : rugged
   b. basic : simple
   c. immoderate : balanced
   d. gleaming : foaming
   e. justified : poetic

5. HEAVY : PONDEROUS

   a. dire : lengthy
   b. gruesome : torn
   c. some : myriad
   d. plastic : gelatinous
   e. lithe : light

WORDS IN CONTEXT

Based on the context in which each **bold** word is used, identify the word usage of each sentence as either C (Correct) or I (Incorrect).

1. Entering the boxing ring, Eric felt intimidated by his fierce-looking opponent.

2. Jim is someone who likes things cut-and-dry, to the point. He is certainly not comfortable with obscurities.

3. Bruce became indigent upon learning that his classmate stole his research project idea.

4. To Helen, Jasmine is a puzzling character. In fact, Jas is an outright obtuse individual.

5. Greek philosophers like Aristotle and Sophocles present some of the most ponderable ideas about human life.

Review Exercises / Lessons 26–30

NAME THAT CLUSTER

To the left of the groups of words, put the Roman numeral that corresponds with these theme (or cluster) titles:

Words Relating to . . .

I. People You will Meet on the SAT I
II. Tricky Twins and Triplets (Words Often Confused)
III. Things of Little Importance or Value
IV. Being Wise and Sharp-Minded

Cluster Title _____   1. shrewd, acute, perspicacious, sagacious, astute

Cluster Title _____   2. virtuoso, skeptic, artisan, hedonist, charlatan

Cluster Title _____   3. petty, trifling, peripheral, negligible, trivial

Cluster Title _____   4. indignant, indigenous, ponderable, ponderous, obtuse, obscure

SENTENCE COMPLETIONS

Read the sentence carefully. Then, from the five vocabulary words given in parentheses, circle the words that *best* completes each of the sentences below.

1. The tropical island's _____ fruits include papaya and mango. Both are readily available and picked fresh daily from the island's bountiful fruit trees.
   (obscure, artisan, indigenous, peripheral, paltry)

2. The _____ sculpted beautiful bowls, pitchers, and vases from clay. The clay took on new life in his hands.
   (virtuoso, charlatan, diva, artisan, ascetic)

3. Your threats do not _____ me, but your boxing gloves do.
   (adversary, intimate, indignant, obscure, intimidate)

4. No experiment could convince the _____ that the scientist
   had discovered a new function of the living cell.
   (skeptic, intimate, indigent, astute, diva, charlatan)

5. _____ activities include thumb-wrestling and bubble-blowing.
   (peripheral, gluttonous, artisan, frivolous, ponderous)

6. Toting a cello and masquerading as a (an) _____, the unusual
   man had no musical talent whatsoever; he was a (an) _____.
   pariah...trifling
   virtuoso...charlatan
   orator...raconteur
   illusion...ambiguity
   atheist...aesthete

7. Todd's _____ mind allowed him to easily discern the difference between consequential matters and _____ issues.
   ascetic...adversarial
   oratory...trifling
   extraneous...incidental
   incisive...petty
   negligible...paltry

8. As his statements became more _____, what he was trying
   to tell us became more _____.
   ambiguous...obscure
   frivolous...indigenous
   irrelevant...aesthetic
   petty...erudite
   sagacious...ambivalent

9. The furniture mover became increasingly _____ when, time
   after time, he simply could not find a way to get the _____
   chest of drawers up the steps and around the tight corner that led
   to the bedroom.
   ambivalent...aesthetic
   paltry...acute
   indigenous...intimidating
   indignant...ponderous
   impudent...trifling

10. Open-minded Hank is far from being a (an) _____; in fact,
    he considers all theories, no matter how far-fetched, _____
    and therefore worthy of his time and consideration.
    ascetic...illusionary
    orator...incidental
    advocate...hedonistic
    intimidator...imprudent
    skeptic...ponderable

ONE DOESN'T BELONG

Three of the words in each grouping relate to each other somehow.
Cross off the one word that does not belong with the others. For a challenge, write the word that does not belong on the line below, and try
your best to define that word. *Note:* Some of the words have been taken
from definitions or exercises that appear within the lessons.

1. paltry   petty   inconsequential   sagacious

   _____ means _____

2. perspicacious   peripheral   prudent   discerning

   _____ means _____

3. virtuoso   artisan   pariah   raconteur

   _____ means _____

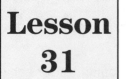

abridge accessible antidote aspire autonomous bolster candor cynical fastidious gratify

---

abridge *vb.* shorten

> This is the **abridged** version of *David Copperfield*. It contains only 200 pages instead of the original 800.

> The school day was **abridged** because teachers were holding parent conferences in the afternoon.

> In order to show the film within the two-hour time slot, it was **abridged**.

accessible *adj.* available; ready for use

> Ramps make the restaurant **accessible** to wheelchair-bound patrons.

> The Hubble telescope has given astronomers **access** to galaxies never seen before.

> Mrs. Kramer is **accessible** to students who need extra help after school.

antidote *n.* something that relieves or prevents; a remedy that counteracts the effects of poison

> Advil is an effective **antidote** for the pain of a torn ligament.

> Acupuncture has been used for centuries as an **antidote** against whatever ails you.

> If an **antidote** for world hunger could be found, Earth would be a more congenial place.

aspire *vb.* to work toward or to have a goal

Vickie **aspires** to be a prima ballerina some day. To dance on the stage is her dream.

Lem **aspired** to go to college out of town, but he couldn't afford anything but the local community college.

If you **aspire** to play hockey for the school, you better practice your skating.

autonomous *adj.* independent

Maggie blossomed once she left home and became **autonomous**.

"With **autonomy** comes responsibility," said the dean.

While others worked on the research in teams, Eddie did the experiments **autonomously**.

bolster *vb.* to support; to strengthen

Pumping iron has **bolstered** Laura's confidence and self-esteem.

A healthy diet **bolsters** your body's resistance to disease.

One's chances of getting into college can be **bolstered** by writing an effective application essay.

candor *n.* honesty, sincerity

"I want complete **candor** from you," said Ms. Flynn. "Is this your own work or is it someone else's?"

Politicians rarely speak with total **candor** because they don't want to offend anyone by revealing how they actually feel about controversial issues.

I know she expects **candor** from me, but if I told her the truth she'd be devastated.

cynical *adj.* believing that all others are motivated by self-interest

As a basically **cynical** person, Holden distrusts everyone he meets.

Jo, a **cynic** to the core, thinks everyone is up to no good.

I'm **cynical** about the overnight change in Louis's personality. He must have an ulterior motive for changing from a thug to a saint.

fastidious *adj.* very attentive to detail; fussy; meticulous

Martha is a **fastidious** homemaker; everything is neat and clean at her house.

A **fastidious** dresser, Annette looks as though she's just stepped out of a fashion magazine.

Juan's homework is **fastidiously** prepared. He takes the time to make it perfect in every way.

gratify *vb.* to please or indulge

Julia **gratifies** her sweet tooth with chocolate Kisses and jelly beans.

I'm pleased that my kid brother gets good grades. It's **gratifying** to see him learning from my mistakes.

The coach, who worked hard to develop his players' skills, was **gratified** by their progress.

MEMORY TIPS

Use these mnemonics (memory devices) to boost your vocabulary. Make up your own memory clues for words in this lesson that are challenging for you. Add these two tips—and your own—to your Vocabulary Notebook.

autonomous As a prefix, *auto-* means *self*. This word really means *self-rule*. Self-rule is essentially independence. Consider these words that contain the prefix *auto-*: automated, automaton, autoimmune, autocrat, automobile. See how *self* plays a role in the meaning of each of these words.

fastidious Let the *f* and *s* sounds at the beginning of this word remind you of *fussy*. Also, remember this vocabulary word's SAT-level synonym, *meticulous*. Like **fastidious**, *meticulous* is an adjective that ends in *-ous* and has four syllables.

MATCHING

Match the vocabulary words in Column A with *one or more* of their defining characteristics appearing in Column B.

Column A

1. bolster *g*
2. autonomous *f*
3. accessible *c*
4. candor *a*
5. abridge *d*
6. aspire *b*
7. fastidious *j*
8. gratify *i*
9. cynical *h*
10. antidote *e*

Column B

a. frankness; forthrightness

b. to have a goal

c. available for use

d. to shorten

e. something that counteracts illness

f. dependent on self

g. to support

h. pessimistic about other people's motives

i. to please

j. fussy

SAT I-STYLE ANALOGIES

First, express a clear and concise relationship between the two given terms. Next, select the pair in the answer choices that *most closely* shares a similar relationship.

1. DEPENDENCE : AUTONOMY

   a. frankness : lethargy
   b. gluttony : sanctuary
   c. avoidance : hindrance
   d. nervousness : composure
   e. friendliness : enthusiasm

2. ANTIDOTE : TOXIN

   a. aspirin : pain
   b. radiation : sunlight
   c. tonic : growth
   d. lotion : skin
   e. mint : herb

3. GRATIFY : PLEASE

   a. annoy : pluck
   b. avoid : evade
   c. lean : spin
   d. tower : fall
   e. splice : dice

4. ELONGATE : ABRIDGE

   a. aggravate : alleviate
   b. truncate : bounce
   c. flip : extend
   d. distend : replete
   e. invade : interfere

5. ATTENTIVE : FASTIDIOUS

   a. happy : gloomy
   b. bored : despondent
   c. frenetic : frantic
   d. worried : confused
   e. firm : stringent

6. BOLSTERING : STURDY

   a. razing : destroyed
   b. tantalizing : jaded
   c. rebuking : spurious
   d. enduring : weak
   e. irrigating : parched

WORDS IN CONTEXT

Based on the context in which each **bold** word is used, identify the word usage as either C (Correct) or I (Incorrect).

1. As her usual **cynical** self, Andrea appreciated the good qualities in all people.

2. The magazine editor asked the writer to **abridge** her column since there wasn't enough space to print the entire piece.

3. Yolanda's compliments certainly **bolstered** Drew's struggling ego.

4. The look and fragrance of aromatherapy candles **gratify** my frazzled senses.

5. Do you **aspire** after a long workout at the gym?

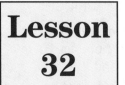

Lesson 32

HOTTEST OF THE HOT WORDS
Letters H to P

**hamper hardy homogeneous integrity intrepid linger lofty
mock nurture opportunist proximity**

---

hamper *vb.* to hinder; to prevent something from happening

Phone calls **hampered** Roger's effort to finish his lab report.

A sore knee **hampered** Jim's rigorous training.

I could not hear what Manuela said. Static **hampered** our phone conversation.

hardy *adj.* healthy and strong; robust

These plants are **hardy**. They'll grow anywhere.

Anyone who can down nine meatballs, a huge bowl of fusilli, and a whole cantaloupe for lunch has to have a **hardy** digestive tract.

The girls are **hardy** enough to withstand a few rain showers during the hike.

homogeneous *adj.* of the same kind; alike; uniform

Of all the states, Utah has the most **homogeneous** population. More than 70 percent of the people are Mormon.

Homogeneous grouping of students according to their ability has long been a sticky issue in public education.

The houses on my block are **homogeneous**. You can hardly tell them apart.

integrity *n.* holding firmly to values, such as honesty; completeness

They called him a man of **integrity** only because no one realized that he was a crook.

The **integrity** of the building was damaged by the earth tremors.

Wallace has no **integrity**. He'll do anything to beat the competition, even break the law if necessary.

intrepid *adj.* fearless

Intrepidly, Columbus sailed west, urging his men to show courage, too.

An **intrepid** stuntman, Steve bravely hurled himself into the ocean far below.

In his youth Matthew was **intrepid**, but as he aged, his innate courage began to falter.

linger *vb.* to hang around; to stay

Maribeth **lingered** after class to talk with the teacher in private.

The smell of Marlene's perfume **lingered** in the room long after she had left.

Daylight **lingers** in the sky past 9 o'clock on summer evenings.

lofty *adj.* very high; towering; grand or noble

Ethan has **lofty** goals. In fact, he expects to be president some day.

Chris's goal is less **lofty**. She hopes to be a schoolteacher.

Marylou dreams **lofty** dreams. I hope she won't be disappointed when reality brings her back to earth.

mock *vb.* to make fun of; to imitate

When Nathan made fun of Sandy, the teacher let him have it: "**Mock** anyone again, Nathan, and your presence in this class is history!"

Mickey's satirical letter to the editor **mocked** the silly new rules in the cafeteria.

Mockingbirds get their name from their ability to imitate, or **mock**, the songs of other birds.

nurture *vb.* to care for, to nourish

The Wild Child is the true story of a boy lost in the woods and **nurtured** by wolves until he was about 12 years old.

Since childhood Julia **nurtured** the idea of becoming a movie star.

In spite of being **nurtured** in a tolerant environment, Kyle became a bigot.

opportunist *n.* a person who seeks self-gain, even at the expense of others, without regard to values or moral principles

Always an **opportunist**, Mac saw Ellen's breakup as a chance to ask her out.

The community thinks the developer is an **opportunist**, more interested in making a dollar than preserving the beauty of the town.

Richie's ambition has made him an **opportunist**. To get ahead he'll do anything, even break the law and hurt others.

proximity *n.* nearness

Because our house is in **proximity** to the airport, I hear planes all day long.

Ally and Julie arranged to get lockers in **proximity** to each other so they could talk between classes.

Please bring me the carton that's standing in **proximity** to the computer station.

MEMORY TIPS

Use these mnemonics (memory devices) to boost your vocabularly. Make up your own memory clues for words in this lesson that are challenging for you. Add these three tips—and your own—to your Vocabulary Notebook.

lofty Do you know what a *loft* is? (Answer: An upper story of a warehouse, a balcony, or an attic.) Well then, a loft is an area that is *up high*. Link this information (information that you already might have known) to the meaning of the adjective, **lofty**.

proximity Link this word to one you already know: ap<u>proxim</u>ately. *Approximately* means *nearly*, which is related to one meaning of **proximity**, *nearness*. Notice how these words share the letters *proxim*. Again, link something you are familiar with to something new, and you will remember the new vocabulary word more readily. Underline <u>proxim</u> when you write <u>proxim</u>ity in your Vocabulary Notebook.

MATCHING

Match the vocabulary words in Column A with *one or more* of their defining characteristics appearing in Column B.

Column A	Column B
1. hamper k	a. healthy
2. intrepid b	b. having no fear
3. proximity g	c. seeker of self-gain
4. nurture i	d. high, high up
5. opportunist c	e. to hang around
6. linger e	f. alike
7. hardy a	g. closeness
8. integrity h	h. sincerity
9. lofty d	i. to care for
10. mock j	j. to ridicule
11. homogeneous f	k. impede

SAT I-STYLE ANALOGIES

First, express a clear and concise relationship between the two given terms. Next, select the pair in the answer choices that *most closely* shares a similar relationship.

1. HECKLER : MOCK

   a. turncoat : trespass
   b. moonlighter : tattle
   c. cartoonist : sketch
   d. relative : laugh
   e. boyfriend : detach

2. HAMPER : IMPEDE

   a. join : cringe
   b. embrace : hug
   c. bring : upgrade
   d. disturb : retaliate
   e. check : skim

3. INTREPID : SUPERHERO

   a. shy : usher
   b. merciful : scientist
   c. grabby : botanist
   d. introverted : recluse
   e. graceful : guitarist

4. DAWDLER : LINGERS

   a. student : judges
   b. hunter : detracts
   c. undertaker : debates
   d. architect : prints
   e. witness : testifies

5. SIMILAR : HOMOGENEOUS

   a. testy : irascible
   b. benevolent : kind
   c. offended : distant
   d. severe : mild
   e. boiling : warm

WORDS IN CONTEXT

Based on the context in which each **bold** word is used, identify the word usage of each sentence as either C (Correct) or I (Incorrect).

1. An animal cell and a plant cell are homogeneous.

2. A daredevil at heart, Gus nicknamed himself "The Intrepid One."

3. Jessie decided that Ben's not returning her phone calls might hamper their relationship.

4. Phil was mocked by his soccer teammates for being the season's most frequent goal-scorer.

5. Lingering in bed in the morning was not Dana's style. Instead, she was up and on the go: on her treadmill for 30 minutes, then e-mailing her coworkers.

Lesson 33

HOTTEST OF THE HOT WORDS

Letters Q to Z

> querulous recount rigor saturate scrutinize surpass
> tentative thrive tranquility uniformity vilify whimsical

querulous *adj.* whining; complaining

The baby gets **querulous** when she's tired. Her crankiness means she needs a nap.

Always whining and complaining **querulously**, Zeena made life miserable for Ethan.

Every time the teacher gives homework the class becomes **querulous**. I've never seen such complainers.

recount *vb.* to tell a story

Let me **recount** what happened in the park on Sunday afternoon. It's a good story.

Grandpa loves to **recount** tales of his carefree youth.

The attorney asked the witness to **recount** what he saw on the evening of May 3rd.

rigor *n.* harshness, severity

Because the course lacks **rigor**, Holly is bored. She'd much prefer a more challenging class.

There's no more **rigorous** event than the Iron Man triathlon—swimming two miles, biking 100 miles, and then running a marathon.

To endure the **rigors** of winter at the South Pole, one needs perseverance and a bit of masochism.

saturate *vb.* to wet or soak completely; to totally fill up

Billy has **saturated** the school with posters for the dance. You can't go anywhere in the building without seeing one.

The web site is **saturated** with ads, so many in fact that they interfere with the purpose of the site.

The field is **saturated**. It's too wet to play on it—game postponed.

scrutinize *vb.* to read or look at very closely and carefully

Gus **scrutinized** the sports section for the scores of yesterday's high school football games, but he couldn't find them no matter how hard he looked.

As we entered the stadium, the ticket takers **scrutinized** our faces as though they were searching for someone in particular.

With a pen in hand, Mr. Harvey **scrutinizes** our writing, looking for mistakes in grammar and usage.

surpass *vb.* to be better than; to excel

The suspense in the movie **surpassed** my expectations. I had no idea that a documentary could be so riveting.

Dad told me that I had long ago **surpassed** him as an athlete and scholar.

Mike ran the marathon not to win the race, but to **surpass** last year's time.

tentative *adj.* hesitant; not definite

Ice-skating is **tentatively** planned for Saturday. If the weather stays cold, we'll go; if it warms up, we'll do something else.

Rose, who is afraid of heights, feels **tentative** about her rock-climbing date with Charles. In fact, the jitters have started.

There's a **tentative** agreement to settle the strike, but the workers must vote first.

thrive *vb.* to grow strong; to flourish

Redwoods **thrive** along the California coast.

Little children **thrive** emotionally with lots of praise and love.

Mr. Kroc built a hamburger stand into a **thriving** business called McDonald's.

tranquility *n.* peacefulness; calmness

Turmoil turned to **tranquility** after the children went to sleep.

Keesha loves to end the day **tranquilly**, with a good book or some soothing music.

The water was so **tranquil** you could see your reflection in it.

uniformity *n.* sameness

The boys were the picture of **uniformity**: All wore oversize pants, long T-shirts, baseball caps, and sneakers.

Carla became depressed over the **uniformity** of her days. She felt as though she were caught in a rut.

Because every day was **uniformly** sunny, Gary yearned for some rain.

vilify *vb.* to slander or defame someone's name

By calling him a "shiftless monster," the principal **vilified** the boy who had pulled the false alarm.

The newspapers **vilified** Patty, but the fact is that she had been falsely charged with the burglary.

Jay Leno and the other late night comedians **vilified** the president for a slip of the tongue.

whimsical *adj.* fanciful

Dave's **whimsical** imagination enables him to tell the most amazing and entertaining stories.

The tale is based on the **whimsical** idea of a man who remains young while his portrait on the wall grows old.

Ms. Scotch declined to accept Nina's **whimsical** excuse for being late. "Sorry," she said, "abduction by extraterrestrials is not an authorized excuse."

MEMORY TIPS

Use these mnemonics (memory devices) to boost your vocabulary. Make up your own memory clues for words in this lesson that are challenging for you. Add this tip—and your own—to your Vocabulary Notebook.

vilify Use this chant to remind you that **vilify** means *to slander or defame someone's name*. "**Vilify** the villain! **Vilify** the villain! **Vilify** the villain!" After all, if someone's name and reputation are to be marred (spoiled), why not the town villain?

MATCHING

Match the vocabulary words in Column A with *one or more* of their defining characteristics appearing in Column B.

Column A

1. recount *g*
2. vilify *i*
3. querulous *l*
4. scrutinize *k*
5. saturate *e*
6. whimsical *a*
7. tranquility *c*
8. uniformity *j*
9. thrive *d*
10. rigor *b*
11. surpass *f*
12. tentative *h*

Column B

a. imaginative
b. hard work
c. calmness
d. grow strongly
e. soak completely
f. to go beyond
g. tell a story
h. hesitant
i. to slander
j. sameness
k. examine closely
l. complaining

SAT I-STYLE ANALOGIES

First, express a clear and concise relationship between the two given terms. Next, select the pair in the answer choices that *most closely* shares a similar relationship.

1. SCRUTINIZE : BROWSE

   a. decorate : impede
   b. snooze : fantasize
   c. leak : ooze
   d. criticize : praise
   e. lift : ebb

2. MOISTEN : SATURATE

   a. adjoin : link
   b. purchase : return
   c. rate : project
   d. address : toil
   e. jog : sprint

3. CONSTELLATIONS : UNIFORMITY

   a. diamonds : pliability
   b. fibers : versatility
   c. whirlpools : exceptionality
   d. watches : dependability
   e. contracts : manageability

4. WHIMSICAL : FANCIFUL

   a. grand : mint
   b. flawed : marred
   c. beige : warm
   d. fluffy : soiled
   e. arched : scrolled

5. HAND GESTURES : RACONTEUR

   a. foot taps : pianist
   b. shoulder shrugs : misanthrope
   c. hand motions : juggler
   d. belly circles : ballerina
   e. knee bends : tailor

WORDS IN CONTEXT

Based on the context in which each **bold** word is used, identify the word usage of each sentence as either C (Correct) or I (Incorrect).

1. Expressing your fashion sense can be achieved through a school
   I dress code of uniformity.

2. Every night Tanya would scrutinize her face for breakouts and
   C blemishes. She'd stay in front of the mirror for close to an hour.

3. Dorothy, a woman who prides herself on her fine reputation, became
   sorrowful when she learned that the town gossip was vilifying her
   C good name.

4. As a mother of five, Ms. Jallow's days are saturated with food shop-
   C ping, doing laundry, and attending to the social calendar.

5. Hannah's whimsical daydreams included dreams of living in Paris
   C and visions of being a famous fashion model.

Lesson 34

MILLENNIUM HOT WORDS

aggregate audacious aviary complementary debunk
discrepancy eclectic excerpt glacial

---

aggregate *n.* a sum total or mixture

Concrete consists of an **aggregate** of sand, gravel, Portland cement, and water.

An **aggregate** of minority groups now makes up the majority of California's population.

An **aggregation** of disgruntled citizens mounted a rebellion against Mayor Meyer and threw out the rascal.

audacious *adj.* very bold

More **audacious** than wise, Marvin daringly told the assistant principal to mind his own business.

In an **audacious** move, Jodi bucked the odds and scored the winning three-pointer at the buzzer.

Juan struck me as a meek and timid fellow. That he is **audacious** enough to wrestle with alligators is amazing.

aviary *n.* an enclosed space for birds

The new **aviary** at the zoo contains 200 different kinds of birds.

As Lucy walked through the **aviary**, a white dove landed on her shoulder.

This **aviary** contains birds of prey. The other one houses songbirds from all over the world.

complementary *adj.* serving to complete another

The couple's talents **complement** each other. She raises vegetables and he cooks them.

The art curriculum includes a course in abstract painting that is **complemented** by a course in realistic drawing and painting.

Our whirlwind visit to dorms and classrooms was **complemented** by a Q and A session in the college chapel.

debunk *vb.* to prove wrong or false

The photo of an alleged UFO was **debunked** by the man who threw a frisbee up in the air for the photographer.

Old wives tales are continuously **debunked** by modern research.

The claim that Mallory reached the summit of Mt. Everest was **debunked** by an analysis of the photos.

discrepancy *n.* a difference

Julian was upset by the **discrepancy** between the amount of the paycheck and what he was told he would earn.

A **discrepancy** in the suspect's story led the detectives to infer that he was lying.

I never fail to find a **discrepancy** in my checkbook between my figures and the bank's figures.

eclectic *adj.* taken from many different sources

On my street the houses are **eclectic**. Each one is built in a different architectural style.

Mom prefers an **eclectic** assortment of furniture, regardless of its condition or style.

This dinner is **eclectic**: egg rolls, borscht, pizza, and crème brûlée for dessert.

excerpt *n.* a portion of a text or musical piece that is taken, or extracted, from the whole

The critical reading section of the SAT I contains short **excerpts** taken from books, periodicals, and speeches.

The medley consists of several **excerpts** from Broadway musical comedies.

In preparing the case, Shazia **excerpted** articles from the U.S. Constitution.

glacial *adj.* very cold or very slow moving (in both cases, like a glacier)

Quentin built his house at a **glacial** pace. It took him 12 years.

The shopkeeper's **glacial** stare made me feel unwelcome, so I left.

Although I wore several layers of clothing, the **glacial** wind chilled me to the bone.

MEMORY TIPS

Use these mnemonics (memory devices) to boost your vocabulary. Make up your own memory clues for words in this lesson that are challenging for you. Add these tips—and your own—to your Vocabulary Notebook.

aggregate Do you remember what the root "gregis" means? Think back to *gregarious*, which appeared in Lesson 6. "Gregis" means *group* or *herd*. So, to **aggregate** is to collect and gather until a *group* is formed.

aviary If you are familiar with the word *aviation* (having to do with airplanes and flying), then you can link this knowledge to **aviary**, a place where birds fly around.

complementary Let the underlined portion of this word lead you to the word's meaning, *to complete*. Your math knowledge could help you here. Remember that **complementary** angles add up to 90 degrees. In a way, these angles *complete* each other in order to reach 90 degrees. Once again, the idea behind this memory tip is linking what you already know to something "new."

excerpt To remember the meaning of this word, it is helpful to know the prefix *ex-*. *Ex-* means "out," just like in e̲xit, e̲xpunge, and e̲xude. The Critical Reading sections of the SAT I-Verbal contain excerpts, pieces of writing taken *out* of the larger piece.

MATCHING

Match the vocabulary words or roots in Column A with *one or more* of their defining characteristics appearing in Column B.

Column A	Column B
1. discrepancy	a. freezing cold
2. audacious	b. enclosed space for birds
3. excerpt	c. a section from a piece of writing
4. aggregate	d. to prove false
5. gregis	e. difference
6. eclectic	f. selected from various, good sources
7. complementary	g. a group or herd
8. aviary	h. bold
9. debunk	i. to gather
10. glacial	j. completing each other

SAT I-STYLE ANALOGIES

First, express a clear and concise relationship between the two given terms. Next, select the pair in the answer choices that *most closely* shares a similar relationship.

1. COLD : GLACIAL

    a. smart : cheerful
    b. brazen : outstripped
    c. lazy : melancholy
    d. chubby : obese
    e. silly : serious

2. EXCERPT : SHORT STORY

    a. paragraph : magazine
    b. headline : play
    c. sentence : byline
    d. inch : mile
    e. circle : essay

3. AGGREGATE : DISPERSE

    a. bleed : imbue
    b. cover : converge
    c. review : standardize
    d. resume : restrict
    e. arrive : depart

4. SKYDIVER : AUDACIOUS

    a. graphic artist : tremendous
    b. gardener : herbal
    c. presenter : bold
    d. protagonist : leading
    e. emperor : colorful

5. DEBUNK : VERIFY

    a. include : exclude
    b. envelope : adhere
    c. label : inscribe
    d. credit : rotate
    e. format : erase

6. AVIARY : ENCLOSURE

    a. church : cathedral
    b. box : container
    c. injury : toxin
    d. flood : landmark
    e. award : conjecture

WORDS IN CONTEXT

Based on the context in which each **bold** word is used, identify the word usage of each sentence as either C (Correct) or I (Incorrect).

1. The aggregate supply of apples picked by the children was more than their parents hoped for: 18 bushels!

2. Dr. Rain became irritated when the science experiment that was supposed to confirm his findings ended up debunking them.

3. Justin excerpted a quoted passage from the novel to demonstrate his theory.

4. Their opinions about weekend plans were complementary, and the two began quarreling into the wee hours of the morning.

5. Mr. Seymor's tie collection is eclectic. He purchases expensive ties in a variety of patterns and materials at upscale boutiques.

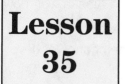

Lesson 35

MORE MILLENNIUM HOT WORDS

insuperable *adj.* unable to be overcome

Playing an **insuperable** team, we don't stand a chance in Saturday's game.

The odds seemed **insuperable**, but survivors were found in the rubble 10 days after the earthquake.

Napoleon's army was **insuperable** until it reached Moscow, where it met defeat.

lithe *adj.* nimble and flexible

Do lots of stretching and stay away from fast food if you really want to be as **lithe** as a willow.

To be a ballerina, you must be lean and **lithe**.

Jason is a walking stiff on stage, but the role calls for an actor with a **lithe** body like Fred Astaire's.

misanthrope *n.* someone who dislikes all people

Hal has a **misanthropic** streak. He dislikes almost everyone.

Claire looks at everyone through rose-colored glasses. A dose of **misanthropy** might give her personality a bit more substance.

Rachel's statement that all men are vermin confirmed her status as a **misanthrope**.

pitfall *n.* an unseen danger, risk, or drawback

The one **pitfall** in Doug's excellent plan is that it may cost too much.

The single **pitfall** Kerry found in going to college in Alaska was how much she missed her high school friends.

Beware of the **pitfalls** of sunbathing, especially the chance of developing skin cancer later in life.

raze *vb.* to tear down; to destroy

The old Victorian house was **razed** to make room for a parking garage.

While **razing** the shed, Vickie made a big mistake. She tore down the walls before dismantling the roof.

During the slum-clearance project, more than 1,000 run-down buildings were **razed**.

replete *adj.* filled-up; overflowing

Morticia cannot tell the truth. Her story is **replete** with outrageous exaggerations.

The new mall is **replete** with shops meant to attract fashion-conscious young women.

Although the film is **replete** with sex and violence, it got a "G" rating.

respite *n.* period of inactivity; a lull; a reprieve

Max's **respites** from work last longer than the work itself. At that rate, he'll never finish painting the room.

The rain took a **respite** at midday and permitted the children to go out and play.

If Holly doesn't take a periodic **respite** while driving long distances, she goes stir crazy.

spurious *adj.* false; counterfeit; lacking logic; specious

In our earth science lab, we had to determine which fossils were genuine and which were **spurious**.

McCall said he was the author of the poem, but his claim was **spurious**. The actual author was McCarthy.

Lewis and Clark discovered that the rumors of an all-water route to the Pacific were **spurious**.

vaporize *vb.* to turn to vapor, foam, or mist

Zap! The space ranger **vaporized** the alien creature into a fine mist.

Who doesn't know that water begins to **vaporize** when it starts to boil?

As the dry ice **vaporized**, the actors on stage disappeared in clouds of smoke.

MEMORY TIPS

Use these mnemonics (memory devices) to boost your vocabulary. Make up your own memory clues for words in this lesson that are challenging for you. Add these tips—and your own—to your Vocabulary Notebook.

misanthrope The root at the center of this word holds part of its meaning. "Anthrop" means *man*. Add the prefix *mis-* (meaning "hatred" in this case), and the full meaning of **misanthrope** becomes clear: "hater of mankind." Additional words containing *anthrop* (man) include: anthropology and philanthropy. (See Lesson 8.)

raze Let the irony of this word work for you. In other words, the meaning of **raze** is the *opposite* of what you'd expect. Since **raze** sounds like *raise*, you might think it has to do with building up or erecting a structure. Instead, **raze** means the opposite: to tear down to the ground.

respite How exciting! The meaning is actually *in the word*. In your Vocabulary Notebook, underline the parts of this word that spell *rest*.

MATCHING

Match the vocabulary words or roots in Column A with *one or more* of their defining characteristics appearing in Column B.

Column A	Column B
1. insuperable	a. filled to the brim
2. vaporize	b. to turn into some sort of mist
3. raze	c. a break in activity
4. pitfall	d. flexible
5. lithe	e. unbeatable
6. respite	f. fake
7. spurious	g. to tear down
8. misanthrope	h. man
9. anthrop	i. person who dislikes others
10. replete	j. a trap or danger

SAT I-STYLE ANALOGIES

First, express a clear and concise relationship between the two given terms. Next, select the pair in the answer choices that *most closely* shares a similar relationship.

1. MISANTHROPE :
   HUMANKIND

   a. manicurist : men
   b. hostess : guests
   c. operator : people
   d. misogynist : women
   e. economist : stockbrokers

2. CONGEAL : VAPORIZE

   a. conquer : catch
   b. resubmit : retire
   c. witness : depress
   d. listen : invite
   e. deplete : replete

3. LITHE : YOGA GURU

   a. official : king
   b. funny : comedian
   c. wily : first mate
   d. presentable : engineer
   e. jarring : translator

4. PITFALL : QUICKSAND

   a. hazard : light
   b. mob : crowd
   c. danger : avalanche
   d. arrest : intoxication
   e. oblivion : rebellion

5. CHAMPION : INSUPERABLE

   a. agent : unexpected
   b. terrorist : estranged
   c. photographer : tardy
   d. passenger : slow
   e. spokesperson : articulate

6. RESPITE : RELIEF

   a. enigma : elucidation
   b. boon : scarcity
   c. cocoon : protection
   d. amplifier : extension
   e. machine : imitation

WORDS IN CONTEXT

Based on the context in which each **bold** word is used, identify the word usage as either C (Correct) or I (Incorrect).

1. Insuperable Ivan is a giant who cannot be overcome.
   C

2. The demolition crew followed their order to raze the shabby building.
   C

3. All the participants praised the plan's major pitfall.
   I

4. It is important for weight lifters to be replete so they can do deep squats while holding 50-pound weights.   I

5. The woman vaporized herself with the latest perfume.
   I

Review Exercises / Lessons 31–35

SENTENCE COMPLETIONS

Read the sentence through carefully. Then from the five vocabulary words given in parentheses, circle the word that fits *best*.

1. Because of the prize fighter's awesome competitive record, his fans called him "The _____."
   (aggregate, eclectic, lofty, insuperable, ponderous)

2. Exotic and tropical birds flew around the _____.
   (nurture, aviary, tentative, abridge, glacial)

3. Unfortunately, television programming is _____ with violence; there seems to be fighting, shooting, or bloodshed on the majority of channels.
   (surpassed, querulous, hampered, intrepid, saturated)

4. Big Ego Bruce _____ on flattery.
   (thrives, vilifies, scrutinizes, razes, pitfalls)

5. Despite Tina and Nick's _____, they did not speak a word to each other.
   (respite, proximity, candor, antidote, autonomy)

6. After 5 long days of sightseeing, the Hillers took a(an) _____ at the hotel pool, where they lounged all day long.
   (raze, linger, mock, respite, excerpt)

7. The aching pit in Ava's stomach served as an _____ sign of something ill-fated to come.
   (opportunist, ominous, inception, aggregate, robust)

8. Chiropractor Rick believes that one of his professional missions is to _____ old wives' tales and replace these spurious theories with sound biological knowledge.
   (vilify, hamper, debunk, scrutinize, nurture)

9. Gretta's supple, _____ body helps her achieve each grace-ful pose on the balance bar and uneven bars.
(lithe, whimsical, thriving, glacial, eclectic)

10. Lacking a green thumb, Jillian selects only the most _____ ferns to keep as houseplants.
(tentative, bolstered, autonomous, hardy, complementary)

MATCHING

How well do you recall what you learned in the Memory Tips sections of the past five lessons? Try this matching exercise to find out.

Column A

1. the prefix *–ex*, as in *ex*punge or *ex*culpate

2. a synonym for meticulous

3. the prefix *auto-*, as in *auto*immune or *auto*mation

4. the Greek root *gregis*

5. aviation

6. the root *anthrop*

Column B

a. a herd or group

b. relating to planes and flying

c. man

d. out

e. fastidious

f. self

Answer Key

LESSON 1

Matching

1. a   2. b   3. c   4. e   5. d

SAT I-Style Analogies

1. a Antonyms
2. b Antonyms
3. e Antonyms
4. d Opposite Characteristic
   A chatterbox is *not* **reticent**;
   A martinet is *not* lax.
5. b Defining Characteristic (Adjective-to-Noun)
   Pithy characterizes a headline (newspaper headline);
   Crunchy characterizes peanut brittle.

Words in Context

1. C   2. I   3. C   4. C   5. I

LESSON 2

Matching

1. e   2. d   3. c   4. a   5. b

SAT I-Style Analogies

1. c Defining Characteristic
   Prattle is childish;
   Grandiloquence is pompous.
2. b Synonyms
3. a Defining Characteristic (Person-to-Adjective)
   A blabbermouth is **voluble**;
   An imp is irritating.
4. e Antonyms
5. b Defining Characteristic
   Eloquence characterizes an orator;
   Ego characterizes a narcissist.

Words in Context

1. I   2. I   3. C   4. C   5. I

LESSON 3

Matching

1. a, b, d   2. b   3. a   4. e   5. c

SAT I-Style Analogies

1. c Synonyms
2. b Antonyms
3. b Defining Characteristic
   Arrogance characterizes a **braggart**;
   Insincerity characterizes a fraud.
4. a Degree of Intensity
   Proud is less intense than **insolent**;
   Firm is less intense than dogmatic.
   Keep in mind the greater than (>)/less than (<) notation (like you use
   in math) when you figure out analogy relationships on the SAT I:
   proud < insolent
   firm < dogmatic
5. d Synonyms

Words in Context

1. I   2. I   3. C   4. C   5. I

LESSON 4

Matching

1. c, b   2. d, f   3. a, e   4. b   5. d, c   6. a, e

SAT I-Style Analogies

1. c Opposite Characteristic
   Something **hackneyed** lacks novelty (newness, freshness);
   Someone glib (gabby, talkative) lacks succinctness (getting to and
   sticking to the point when speaking or writing).
2. a Defining Characteristic
   A dull saying is a **platitude**;
   A dull expression is a banality.
3. c Defining Characteristic
   A copycat speaks **clichés**;
   An autocrat (a ruler with total power) speaks admonitions (strong
   warnings).
4. a Antonyms
5. b Antonyms

Words in Context

1. I   2. I   3. I   4. C   5. I

LESSON 5

Matching

1. e   2. b   3. a   4. d   5. b

SAT I-Style Analogies

1. a Synonyms
2. c Antonyms
3. e Person-to-Action
   A mediator (a middle person who resolves conflicts and disputes) **mitigates**;
   A runner sprints.
4. e Antonyms
5. e Synonyms

Words in Context

1. I   2. C   3. C   4. I   5. C

REVIEW EXERCISES—LESSONS 1–5

Name That Cluster

1. V   2. III   3. II   4. I   5. IV

Sentence Completions

1. reticence
2. presumptuous
3. egoist
4. vapid
5. concise
6. mitigate . . . alleviated
7. laconic . . . voluble

One Doesn't Belong

1. Garrulous means talkative.
2. Swagger means to walk in a showy way.
3. Taciturn means silent.
4. Allay means to alleviate fear.
5. Palliate means to alleviate, soothe.

LESSON 6

Matching

1. a   2. d   3. b   4. c   5. e

SAT I-Style Analogies

1. b Antonyms
2. d Defining Characteristic
   Amiable characterizes a crony (friend);
   Impassive characterizes a stoic (a person who shows little or no emotion).
3. e Defining Characteristic
   Gregarious characterizes a party animal;
   Fledgling (inexperienced) characterizes a young trainee.
4. a Antonyms
5. c Defining Characteristic
   A jester (clown) is **jocular**;
   A scoundrel (crook, rascal) is crooked (dishonest, corrupt).

Words in Context

1. I   2. C   3. C   4. I   5. I

LESSON 7

Matching

1. b, d   2. e   3. c   4. b   5. a

SAT I-Style Analogies

1. a Antonyms
2. a Opposite Characteristic
   Manners do *not* characterize someone who is **predatory**;
   Jitters (nervous shakes) do *not* characterize someone who is calm.
3. e Defining Characteristic
   Someone **polemical** likes debate;
   Someone erudite (scholarly) likes learning.
4. a Antonyms
5. a Defining Characteristic (Person-to-Adjective)
   A wrangler (fighter) is **disputatious**;
   A bumpkin (country dweller) is rustic (country-like, unrefined).

Words in Context

1. I   2. C   3. C   4. C   5. I

LESSON 8

Matching

1. a   2. e   3. b   4. c   5. c, d

SAT I-Style Analogies

1. c Defining Characteristic
   A **philanthropist** is **altruistic**;
   A corpse (dead body) is lifeless.
2. e Synonyms
3. b Defining Characteristic (Adjective-to-Person)
   Prodigal characterizes a wastrel (a person who wastes, overspends);
   Angel-like characterizes a cherub (plump angel).
4. a Antonyms
5. d Defining Characteristic
   Benevolent characterizes a benediction (a blessing);
   Kind characterizes a compliment (flattering remark).

Words in Context

1. I   2. I   3. C   4. C   5. C

LESSON 9

Matching

1. e, b   2. d   3. c   4. b   5. a

SAT I-Style Analogies

1. b Antonyms
2. a Defining Characteristic
   A **miser** is **austere**;
   A renegade (traitor) is disloyal.
3. e Antonyms
4. c Antonyms
5. c Defining Characteristic
   One who hoards (keeps money, etc., to himself) is **parsimonious**;
   One who discriminates (chooses carefully) is selective.
6. e Degree of Intensity
   Thrifty is less intense than **parsimonious**;
   Sweet is less intense than mawkish.

Words in Context

1. I   2. I   3. C   4. C   5. C

LESSON 10

Matching

1. d   2. a   3. c   4. b   5. e

SAT I-Style Analogies

1. c Defining Characteristic (Noun-to-Adjective)
   A secret code is **cryptic**;
   A memoir story is personal.
2. e Defining Characteristic (Noun-to-Adjective)
   A **quandary** is befuddling;
   A diversion is amusing.
3. c Degree of Intensity
   A flame is less intense than a **conflagration**;
   A trench is less intense than a gorge (big, deep crack in the earth).
4. b Synonyms
5. d Synonyms

Words in Context

1. I   2. I   3. C   4. C   5. C

REVIEW EXERCISES—LESSONS 6–10

Name That Cluster

1. III   2. II   3. V   4. IV   5. I

Sentence Completions

1. austerity
2. gregarious
3. contentious
4. precarious
5. levity
6. jocular . . . cantankerous
7. conflagration . . . adversity

One Doesn't Belong

1. Altruistic means kind, generous toward humankind.
2. Conundrum means a riddle.
3. Squander means to waste time or money.
4. Mercenary means seeking self-gain.
5. Conflagration means an inferno.

LESSON 11

Matching

1. e   2. c   3. d   4. a   5. b

SAT I-Style Analogies

1. c Defining Characteristic
   Deleterious characterizes a toxin (poison);
   Rhythmic characterizes a song.
2. c Antonyms
3. a Antonyms
4. d Defining Characterisitc
   Odious characterizes murder;
   Illusory characterizes magic.
5. e Defining Characteristic (Person-to-Adjective)
   A villain is **nefarious**;
   A dynamo (energetic person) is vivacious (full of life).

Words in Context

1. C   2. I   3. C   4. C   5. I

LESSON 12

Matching

1. c   2. b   3. d   4. a   5. e

SAT I-Style Analogies

1. b Antonyms
2. d Antonyms
3. c Synonyms
4. b Synonyms
5. e Antonyms

Words in Context

1. I   2. I   3. C   4. C   5. I

LESSON 13

Matching

1. b   2. a, c, e   3. a   4. a, b, e   5. d

SAT I-Style Analogies

1. b Antonyms
2. c Opposite Characteristic
   A zealot (great fan or enthusiast) is *not* **indifferent**;
   A guru (expert) is *not* uninformed.
3. a Antonyms
4. c Defining Characteristic
   Detached characterizes a bystander (nonparticipating observer);
   Pious (religious) characterizes a friar.
5. e Antonyms

Words in Context

1. I   2. C   3. I   4. C   5. C

LESSON 14

Matching

1. c   2. d   3. a   4. b   5. e

SAT I-Style Analogies

1. b Antonyms
2. c Opposite Characteristic (Person-to-Adjective)
   A **nomad** (wanderer) is *not* sedentary;
   An imposter (person in disguise) is *not* known.
3. e Cause and Effect (in Reverse Order)
   Something **soporific** makes you drowsy (sleepy);
   Something frigid makes you cold.
4. d Antonyms
5. b Antonyms

Words in Context

1. C   2. I   3. I   4. C   5. C

LESSON 15

Matching

1. d   2. b   3. e   4. c   5. a

SAT I-Style Analogies

1. e Antonyms
2. c Defining Characteristic
   Someone **fawning** is likely to comply (agree, give in);
   Someone mystifying is likely to bewilder (puzzle, confuse).
3. d Defining Characteristic (Person-to-Adjective)
   A slave is characterized as **submissive**;
   A sleepyhead is characterized as drowsy (sleepy).
4. d Defining Characteristic (Adjective-to-Person)
   Servile characterizes a **toady**;
   Powerful characterizes a magnate (powerful businessperson).
5. d Defining Characteristic (Person-to-Adjective)
   A peon is **subservient**;
   A newborn is inexperienced.

Words in Context

1. I   2. I   3. I   4. C   5. C

REVIEW EXERCISES—LESSONS 11–15

Name That Cluster

1. II   2. I   3. V   4. III   5. IV

Sentence Completions

1. sedentary
2. sluggish
3. submissive
4. fawning
5. nefarious
6. lethargic . . . sedentary
7. apathetic . . . avid

One Doesn't Belong

1. Iniquitous means wicked.
2. Subordinate means acting inferior to another.
3. Impassive means without emotion.
4. Obsequious means acting in a slavish fashion.
5. Berate means to scold harshly.

LESSON 16

Matching

1. c, e   2. a, b, d   3. a   4. c, e   5. b, d

SAT I-Style Analogies

1. c Defining Characteristic (Adjective-to-Person/Animal)
   Avid characterizes a devotee (a big fan);
   Nocturnal characterizes an owl.
2. c Synonyms
3. b Synonyms
4. d Defining Characteristic (Person-to-Adjective)
   A dynamo is **exuberant**;
   A subordinate is inferior.
5. e Antonyms

Words in Context

1. I   2. I   3. I   4. C   5. C

LESSON 17

SAT I-Style Analogies

1. c Antonyms
2. e Antonyms
3. b Defining Characteristic (Animal-to-Adjective)
   A mule is **obstinate**;
   A fox is sly.
4. a Synonyms
5. e Synonyms

Words in Context

1. C   2. I   3. I   4. I   5. C

LESSON 18

Matching

1. e   2. d   3. b   4. a   5. c   6. f

SAT I-Style Analogies

1. b Synonyms
2. a Defining Characteristic (Adjective-to-Person)
   Vociferous characterizes rioters;
   Vindictive characterizes avengers.
3. e Defining Characteristic (Noun-to-Adjective)
   A squeal is **strident**;
   An uproar is loud.
4. c Antonyms
5. a Relating Factor
   Acoustics relates to sound quality;
   Gymnastics relates to body movements.

Words in Context

1. C   2. C   3. C   4. I   5. C

LESSON 19

Matching

1. b   2. e   3. d   4. f   5. c   6. a

SAT I-Style Analogies

1. b Degree of Intensity
   Revere is more intense than praise;
   Abhor is more intense than detest.
2. e Defining Characteristic (Person-to-Action Verb)
   A sychophant will **adulate**;
   An altruist will donate.
3. a Whole-to-Part
   A **eulogy** is composed of words;
   A melody is composed of notes.
4. c Antonyms
5. b Synonyms

Words in Context

1. C   2. C   3. I   4. C   5. C

LESSON 20

Matching

1. c   2. b, e   3. a   4. d   5. d

SAT I-Style Analogies

1. a Antonyms
2. d Synonyms
3. e Anonyms
4. e Antonyms
5. c Defining Characteristic (Example-to-Adjective)
   A great amount is **ample**;
   An uphill climb is arduous (hard to do, strenuous).

Words in Context

1. I   2. C   3. C   4. I   5. C

REVIEW EXERCISES—LESSONS 16–20

Name That Cluster

1. IV   2. II   3. V   4. I   5. III

Sentence Completions

1. venerated
2. ebullient
3. mellifluous
4. din
5. avid
6. discordant . . . mellifluous
7. lavish . . . obstinate

One Doesn't Belong

1. Vociferous means loud in terms of talking noisily.
2. Effervescent means bubbly and lively.
3. Defiant means disobedient.
4. Recalcitrant means defiant, stubborn.
5. Surfeit means an oversupply or surplus.

LESSON 21

Matching

1. c   2. e   3. f   4. a   5. d   6. b

SAT I-Style Analogies

1. a Synonyms
2. c Defining Characteristic
   A love of food defines the **glutton**;
   A love of travel defines the voyager.
3. b Antonyms
4. e Relating Factor
   Nourishment has a necessary and definite
   relationship to **alimentary**;
   Purity has a necessary and definite
   relationship to pristine (pure).
5. e Antonyms

Words in Context

1. I   2. I   3. C   4. C   5. C

LESSON 22

Matching

1. d   2. h   3. g, a   4. c
5. e   6. f   7. b   8. h

SAT I-Style Analogies

1. d Antonyms
2. d Relating Factor
   A person who is **scrupulous** has morality;
   A person who is appreciative has gratitude.
3. b Defining Characteristic (Person-to-Adjective)
   A night watchman is **vigilant**;
   A ballerina is graceful.
4. b Relating Factor
   A **conscientious** person conducts himself with a great deal of principle;
   A competitive person conducts himself with a great deal of effort.
5. e Antonyms

Words in Context

1. C   2. I   3. I   4. C   5. C

LESSON 23

Matching

1. e   2. e   3. c   4. a   5. b, d

SAT I-Style Analogies

1. c Defining Characteristic (Person-to-Adjective)
   A rolling stone (person who moves from place to place) is **nomadic**;
   A soul mate (the love of someone's life) is beloved.
2. d Antonyms
3. d Synonyms
4. c Defining Characteristic (Noun-to-Adjective)
   A passing moment is **fleeting**;
   A sad occasion is somber.
5. e Defining Characteristic (Person-to-Adjective)
   A tenant (one who rents a place to live) is **transient**;
   An expert is competent (highly-skilled; proficient).

Words in Context

1. C   2. C   3. C   4. I   5. C

LESSON 24

Matching

1. e   2. f   3. g   4. c   5. a   6. d   7. b

SAT I-Style Analogies

1. d Antonyms
2. e Synonyms
3. a Opposite Characteristic
   A dull speaker is *not* **innovative**;
   An unenthusiastic speaker is *not* lively.
4. b Defining Characteristic (Adjective-to-Example)
   Novel characterizes a novelty item;
   Playful characterizes a bouncing puppy.
5. e Defining Characteristic (Object-to-Adjective)
   An invention is **unprecedented**;
   A thesis is arguable.
6. c Type or example.
   An old Grecian urn is an example (or type) of relic.
   A tuxedo is an example (or type) of attire.

Words in Context

1. C   2. C   3. I   4. C   5. I

LESSON 25

SAT I-Style Analogies

1. a Antonyms
2. d Antonyms
3. d Defining Characteristic (Animal-to-Adjective)
   A fox is **sly**;
   A tortoise is slow.
4. d Defining Characteristic (Adjective-to-Person)
   Stealthy characterizes a private investigator;
   Pious (religious) characterizes a reverend.
5. e Opposite Characteristic
   A skyscraper is *not* **unobtrusive**;
   Glass is *not* opaque.

Words in Context

1. I   2. C   3. C   4. I   5. I

REVIEW EXERCISES—LESSONS 21–25

Name That Cluster

1. IV   2. II   3. III   4. V   5. I

Sentence Completions

1. transient
2. culinary
3. gluttonous
4. conscientious
5. palatable
6. surreptitious . . . covert
7. spectacle . . . inconspicuous

One Doesn't Belong

1. Savory means tasty.
2. Furtive means sneaky, sly.
3. Antediluvian means very, very old.
4. Evanescent means short-lived.
5. Obsolete means outdated, no longer in use.

LESSON 26

Matching

1. e   2. b   3. d   4. a   5. c   6. f

SAT I-Style Analogies

1. c Defining Characteristic
   An **orator** is a very talented speaker;
   A **virtuoso** is a very talented musician.
2. a Defining Characteristic
   Having qualms (doubts) characterizes a **skeptic**;
   Having reveries (daydreams) characterizes a daydreamer.
3. e Synonyms
4. c Antonyms
5. d Action-to-Person
   People ostracize a **pariah**;
   People (tend to) avoid a troublemaker.
6. c Worker to his or her product.
   An **artisan** makes a handicraft.
   A baker makes a pastry.
7. c Person to his or her physical place.
   An **orator** speaks from a pulpit (a raised platform).
   A circus clown performs from within a circus tent.

Words in Context

1. I   2. I   3. C   4. C   5. C

LESSON 27

Matching

1. c   2. a, d   3. b, a   4. a, d   5. e

SAT I-Style Analogies

1. b Antonyms
2. d Synonyms
3. b Defining Characteristic (Adjective-to-Noun)
   Petty characterizes trivia;
   Sour characterizes lemons.
4. a Synonyms
5. b Defining Characteristic (Persons-to-Adjective)
   Fair-weather friends are **superficial**;
   Unruly motorists are perilous.

Words in Context

1. C   2. C   3. I   4. C   5. C

LESSON 28

Matching

1. c, d   2. a   3. d   4. b   5. e

SAT I-Style Analogies

1. d Antonyms
2. a Defining Characteristic (Person-to-Adjective)
   An originator is characterized as **ingenious**;
   A flame eater is characterized as daring.
3. b Relating Factor
   Being **judicious** is related to fairness;
   Being tactful is related to finesse.
4. d Defining Characteristic (Adjective-to-Person)
   Shrewd characterizes a wise person;
   Egotistical characterizes a braggart.
5. a Synonyms

Words in Context

1. C   2. I   3. C   4. I   5. C

LESSON 29

Matching

1. d   2. e   3. c   4. a   5. b

SAT I-Style Analogies

1. d Change of State
   When divergent things come together, they **coalesce**;
   When disparate (separate) things come together, they converge (combine).
2. b Defining Characteristic (Person-to-Adjective)
   An aesthete is **aesthetic**;
   An imp (pesty child) is mischievous.
3. d Synonyms
4. e Person-to-Purpose (expressed as an action verb)
   A doctor helps people to **convalesce**;
   A tour guide helps people to sightsee.
5. b Type-to-Example
   A type of **illusion** is a hallucination;
   A type of pant is boot-cut.

Words in Context

1. I   2. I   3. C   4. C   5. C

LESSON 30

Matching

1. f   2. c   3. a   4. b   5. e   6. d   7. g

SAT I-Style Analogies

1. e Synonyms
2. c Opposite Characteristic
   A millionaire is not **indigent**;
   A big mouth (big talker) is not mute (silent.)
3. e Defining Characteristic (Adjective-to-Person)
   Impudent characterizes an imp (impish, misbehaved youth);
   Lifeless characterizes a corpse (dead body).
4. c Antonyms
5. c Degree of Intensity
   Heavy is less intense than **ponderous**;
   Some is less intense than myriad (a great number).

Words in Context

1. C   2. C   3. I   4. I   5. C

REVIEW EXERCISES—LESSONS 26–30

Name That Cluster

1. IV   2. I   3. III   4. II

Sentence Completions

1. indigenous
2. artisan
3. intimidate
4. skeptic
5. Frivolous
6. virtuoso . . . charlatan
7. incisive . . . petty
8. ambiguous . . . obscure
9. indignant . . . ponderous
10. skeptic . . . ponderable

One Doesn't Belong

1. Sagacious means wise.
2. Peripheral means unimportant, or not central to main point.
3. Pariah means a social outcast.

LESSON 31

Matching

1. g	2. f	3. c	4. a	5. d
6. b	7. j	8. i	9. h	10. e

SAT I-Style Analogies

1. d Antonyms
2. a Cause and Effect
   An **antidote** lessens the effect of a toxin (poison);
   Aspirin lessens the effect of pain.
3. b Synonyms
4. a Antonyms
5. e Degree of Intensity
   Attentive (to detail) is less intense than **fastidious**;
   Firm (in terms of discipline) is less intense than stringent (strict).
6. a Cause and Effect
   Bolstering results in something becoming sturdy;
   Razing results in something being destroyed.

Words in Context

1. I   2. C   3. C   4. C   5. I

LESSON 32

Matching

1. k   2. b   3. g   4. i   5. c   6. e

7. a   8. h   9. d   10. j   11. f

SAT I-Style Analogies

1. c Person-to-Action
   A heckler will likely **mock**;
   A cartoonist will likely sketch.
2. b Synonyms
3. d Defining Characteristic (Adjective-to-Person)
   Intrepid characterizes a superhero;
   Introverted (keeping to oneself) characterizes a recluse (a person who keeps to himself; a hermit).
4. e Person-to-Action
   A dawdler **lingers**;
   A witness testifies.
5. a Degree of Intensity
   Similar is less alike than **homogeneous** (identical);
   Testy is less anger-driven than irascible (easily angered).

Words in Context

1. I   2. C   3. C   4. I   5. C

LESSON 33

Matching

1. g	2. i	3. l	4. k	5. e	6. a
7. c	8. j	9. d	10. b	11. f	12. h

SAT I-Style Analogies

1. d Antonyms
2. e Degree of Intensity
   To moisten is less intense than to **saturate**;
   A jog is less intense than a sprint.
   Or, think of it this way:
   moisten < **saturate**
   jog < sprint
3. a Opposite Characteristic
   Constellations lack **uniformity**;
   Diamonds lack pliability.
4. b Synonyms
5. c Tool-to-Person
   Hand gestures is a "tool" that a **raconteur** (storyteller) is likely to use;
   Hand motions is a "tool" that a juggler is likely to use.

Words in Context

1. l	2. C	3. C	4. C	5. C

LESSON 34

Matching

1. e	2. h	3. c	4. i	5. g
6. f	7. j	8. b	9. d	10. a

SAT I-Style Analogies

1. d Degree of Intensity
   Cold is less intense than **glacial**;
   Chubby is less intense than obese.
2. a Part-to-Whole
   An **excerpt** is a small written piece taken from a short story (for example);
   A paragraph is a small written portion taken from a magazine (for example).
3. e Antonyms
4. d Defining Characteristic
   A skydiver is characterized as **audacious**;
   A protagonist (lead/main character from a story) is characterized as leading.
5. a Antonyms
6. b Type Relationship
   An **aviary** is a type of enclosure;
   A box is a type of container.

Words in Context

1. C	2. C	3. C	4. I	5. C

LESSON 35

Matching

1. e	2. b	3. g	4. j	5. d
6. c	7. f	8. i	9. h	10. a

SAT I-Style Analogies

1. d Defining Characteristic
   A **misanthrope** dislikes humankind;
   A misogynist dislikes women in particular.
2. e Antonyms
3. b Defining Characteristic (Adjective-to-Person)
   Lithe characterizes a yoga guru (yoga expert);
   Funny characterizes a comedian.
4. c Category-to-Example
   An example of a **pitfall** is quicksand;
   An example of a danger is an avalanche (landslide).
   Notice that the latter terms (quicksand and avalanche) are both natural disasters.
5. e Defining Characteristic (Person-to-Adjective)
   A champion is **insuperable**;
   A spokesperson is articulate (well-spoken; eloquent).
6. c Purpose Relationship
   The purpose of a **respite** is relief;
   The purpose of a cocoon is protection.

Words in Context

1. C	2. C	3. I	4. I	5. I

REVIEW EXERCISES—LESSONS 31–35

Sentence Completions

1. Insuperable
2. aviary
3. saturated
4. thrives
5. proximity
6. respite
7. ominous
8. debunk
9. lithe
10. hardy

Matching

1. d   2. e   3. f   4. a

5. b   6. c

Appendix A
Mini–Vocabulary Clusters

Vocabulary is important not only for SAT I preparation but also for life-long writing and speaking skill. The bold titles, as shown below, could suffice as basic definitions. However, to get a sense of each word's particular usage, you should consult a dictionary or *Webster.com*. Each word also has its subtleties and nuances of meaning, which you can best understand through reading and hearing the word used correctly.

As you enrich your vocabulary, you will become a more eloquent speaker and a more competent writer. This revised edition of *Hot Words for the SAT I* presents a plethora of bonus words to you.

High Point
acme
apex
apogee
peak
pinnacle
summit
zenith

Low Point
abyss
chasm
gorge
nadir

Prevent or Frustrate a Plan
deter
foil
hamper
hinder
impede
obstruct

preclude
stymie
thwart

Confuse
baffle
befuddle
bemuse
confound
perplex

Erase, Void, Get Rid Of
abolish
abrogate
annihilate
annul
efface
eradicate
expunge
nullify
obliterate
vanquish
void

Beginner
amateur
apprentice
fledgling
neophyte
novice
rookie
tyro

Small Amount or Quantity
dearth
deplete
devoid
paucity
scarcity
sparse

Lie or Stretch the Truth
embroider
fabricate
prevaricate

Rest Period or Break
cessation
hiatus
lull
moratorium
reprieve
respite
siesta

Appendix B
More Tricky Twins

My experience as a verbal tutor reveals to me—time and again—how even the most conscientious students can easily confuse words. Even honors students regularly confuse words that sound alike or words that look similar. That is why this second edition of *Hot Words for the SAT I* includes even more tricky twins (beyond Lessons 29 and 30). Challenge yourself to learn the different meanings and to master the spelling of these tricky twins.

Remember how effective flash cards, sticky notes, and daily review can be.

adept—skilled; competent
inept—unskilled; incompetent

amity—friendship; trust
enmity—hatred; bitter feeling

avert—turn away
divert—amuse; entertain

bemoan—lament
bemuse—confuse; befuddle

capacious—spacious; having large capacity
rapacious—greedy; grasping

enervate—weaken
venerate—respect

effervescent—bubbly
evanescent—short-lived

flounder—plunge about, as if in quicksand
founder—fail; sink

hail—cheer for; acclaim
hale—healthy

impassive—apathetic; indifferent
impassioned—ardent; fervent

ingenious—creative
ingenuous—honest

invective—a vicious, verbal attack; tirade
inventive—creative; resourceful

lucid—clear; transparent
lurid—gruesome; violent

paramount—of greater value
tantamount—of equal value

picaresque—relating to adventure stories about rogues
picturesque—scenic

prodigal—wasteful
prodigious—very large

provincial—narrow-minded
providential—saving for future

solicitude—concern
solitude—aloneness

temerity—reckless boldness
timidity—shyness

tonic—an invigorating drink
toxic—poisonous

voluble—talkative
voluminous—very large

Word Index

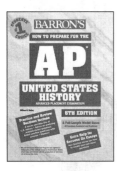